MW01518705

Rosanna,
Enjoy!
take care!
-8
Shay

Worthy 2.0

The Journey of Finding HER
(A Black Sheep Manifesto)

Shaynicorn

BALBOA.PRESS
A DIVISION OF HAY HOUSE

This book is a work of non-fiction. Unless otherwise noted, the author and the publisher make no explicit guarantees as to the accuracy of the information contained in this book and in some cases, names of people and places have been altered to protect their privacy.

Balboa Press books may be ordered through booksellers or by contacting:

Balboa Press
A Division of Hay House
1663 Liberty Drive
Bloomington, IN 47403
www.balboapress.com
844-682-1282

Because of the dynamic nature of the Internet, any web addresses or links contained in this book may have changed since publication and may no longer be valid. The views expressed in this work are solely those of the author and do not necessarily reflect the views of the publisher, and the publisher hereby disclaims any responsibility for them.

The author of this book does not dispense medical advice or prescribe the use of any technique as a form of treatment for physical, emotional, or medical problems without the advice of a physician, either directly or indirectly. The intent of the author is only to offer information of a general nature to help you in your quest for emotional and spiritual well-being. In the event you use any of the information in this book for yourself, which is your constitutional right, the author and the publisher assume no responsibility for your actions.

Print information available on the last page.

ISBN: 979-8-7652-4734-1 (sc)
ISBN: 979-8-7652-4735-8 (hc)
ISBN: 979-8-7652-4733-4 (e)

Library of Congress Control Number: 2023922056

Balboa Press rev. date: 02/28/2024

For Every Little Girl,
For Her Sisters,
For Her Tribe,
For Her

Contents

Foreword

Once Upon a Time, an Evil Queen, a Court Jester, and a Narcissist told a little Princess she wouldn't amount to anything on her own. Fast forward, that Princess grew into a Queen who is now straightening her crown while sipping her tea, building her empire she made on her own. Buckle up sweetheart, she's just getting started on her happily ever after, leaving those foolish mortals behind. This is her story.

A Note from the Author

On occasion, I'll reread the words I wrote while under the spell of believing the story written is worth sharing. An encapsulating heroine who rarely looks in the mirror and appreciates the unlikelihood of standing where she does today. The message was quite clear of what needed to be done- "stand in your power and speak your truth." This is what my healer told me. She told me that I don't live there anymore. And when I'm done, I hope you will understand that this was only ever about healing. For it was foretold long ago that I would break the cycle.

You are the writer of your story.
I was a victim of physical, emotional, and psychological abuse.
I am disabled.
I was ashamed.
But now,
I am a Trauma Survivor.
I am a Fibromyalgia Warrior.
I am a Disability Advocate.
I am an unapologetic, powerful human being
taking up the space I deserve and earned.
The past no longer defines me, but it made me.
I am a badass.
So be it, so it is.

PS: Please buy my book so I can afford to see The Eras Tour.

Trigger Warning

"Shame dies when stories are told in safe spaces."- Ann Voscamp

THERE ARE A LOT OF SELF-HELP BOOKS OUT THERE. STORIES FULL OF ways to cope and overcome. When we are desperate, we look outside of ourselves for help. We hope to find answers as if a perfect manual exists to guide us back to life the way it was before the trauma happened. The trauma that changed our lives. Sometimes we don't even realize how traumatic something really was until much later in our lives. When you're an adult, you don't have a choice. You have to face the world, be productive, pretend to be happy, or even pretend to be normal- whatever that is.

I can't promise this book will change your life, but I can share how my life has changed. I can share the healing model I've developed over my evolution of going from an abused, perfectionist, angel child who was afraid of everything to who I am today- still a little damaged, still a little broken- but free. If anything, even if the model doesn't resonate with you- I hope you feel hope from the words of my truth that there is freedom from the pain, the trauma, and the past. We don't have to live there anymore was one of the most profound statements my healer shared with me. I want to help your healing process so that you don't have to live there anymore either. Take my hand, and let's walk through this journey together.

I want to warn you. This book may have some triggering passages for you. It reflects my pain, my trauma, my depression, my fibromyalgia- but it also represents so much more. It gives you my hope, my passion, my tenacity, and my belief that things can always get better.

I am not sorry to tell my story. I am not sorry for taking up space in this world. That being said, each of the phases of my healing process require looking deep within. The journal passages you will see from roughly ages 10 until now are full of darkness, particularly in the trauma and grief sections.

The intention of the writing is to not trigger you, but to make you feel seen and feel not so alone. To let you know that others may feel this way from time to time, and that's okay. We have to hold space for the moments when we struggle, yet also celebrate the moments we move forward in our healing journeys.

This is what I hope to give you as you walk through the chaos of a healing journey that has been anything but linear. Each section will proceed out of order intentionally, just like in real life as we try to climb out of dark places. I hope that if you are currently living in a dark place, this book helps you to climb out of it, or better yet- find your wings and fly.

I am honored to have you here with me, waiting to take off. Thank you for being my wingman, woman, or person as I tell my story. All humans are welcome here. May this be a safe space for you.

LET'S GO

I'm really doing it.
I waited long enough.
I was afraid before.
I no longer carry the burden of fear.
I carry a fire.
It goes out sometimes.
Only to be reborn.
For all good things come to an end.
Just like every cycle of life.
The next version is not afraid.
The next version is not on fire.
The next version is the fire.
The path was always lit.
She was just finding the way to HER.
Finding HER next best version.
The last version has come to an end.

#Worthy2.0

The High Road

WORTHY: A WORD DEFINED BY APPROVAL OF OTHERS. PERHAPS, YOU are worthy of an award, an accommodation, or a title. Worthy means you are deserving of an honor. What about your self-worth? Who defines that? They say your self-esteem and self-confidence. Being worthy means you have an unshakable belief in yourself and that if you work hard enough, you deserve all the accomplishments that come to you. That you have pride and dignity that you carry with you. You don't have to have a big ego to be worthy or project one. Your self-worth is driven by your opinion of yourself.

In today's world, it can be hard to feel worthy. Little girls who see size zero models on television and social media and may think they aren't worthy if they don't look like them. Little boys are taught to be tough and not cry no matter what, even if they are getting bullied at school. People can be cruel and you are told to be hard. You are told to hide your emotions. That's what I did. That's why I started journaling at a young age. When I look at my oldest journals starting in middle school, I am so sorry for that little girl. She was hurting. She was depressed. And she didn't know how to ask for help. She was too afraid to.

I've wasted a lot of time living in a place that was not where I belonged, so much so I didn't really want to be here. I hated my life. As a matter of fact, I wanted it to end on numerous occasions. I was obese not realizing why I was so sick as a child. I was extremely prone to illness and spent many days out of school. I wanted to be an athlete and my body didn't want to cooperate and it felt like no one wanted to help figure it all out. I certainly didn't understand why I couldn't keep up with others.

Then something changed. In 2019, I made a lot of big life changes. I was living on my own for the first time, feeling like I needed to hide from the world after feeling uncomfortably exposed. A few months before, I had a severe reaction to emotional and verbal abuse. My legs started generating all these red blobs all over my legs. I did not know what was happening. I thought maybe, finally, I was going to be put out of my misery.

Instead it led me down a journey of a fibromyalgia diagnosis. Fibromyalgia affects millions of people and still has no cure. It is a label you're given when they can't quite figure out what is wrong with you. It has hundreds of symptoms, but for me the worst ones were the fatigue, the migraines, and the flaring. Flaring is different from person to person. Mine feels like a burning sensation that typically starts in my arms and can trickle down, depending on the intensity, to my legs and torso. I have extremely poor temperature control and can easily become hot or cold. I can sweat through my clothes when flaring, which can be particularly embarrassing if I'm in public. My period pain is more substantial than a normal female- which is already bad enough in itself. And my goodness, can I get dizzy. I have passed out in public more times than I would like to admit.

You might ask- what causes fibromyalgia? Researchers from the Mayo Clinic believe it to be triggered from either a traumatic event or prolonged psychological stress. For me, I had endured psychological abuse for the majority of my life, but in this case, it was the trauma of realizing the difficult decision of cutting off toxic people. The kind of people who should not be toxic. The kind who are supposed to play an integral part of your life. But they weren't good for me. They were causing all these health issues at hand. And finally when it was stated out loud "we won't bother you anymore"- despite this being exactly what I wanted, it was traumatic. It was something to grieve.

That year I had a lot to grieve. I also lost one of my best friends at the age of 30. It was completely unexpected. These events led me to create the four steps of healing that you will pass through with me on this journey. But the universe wasn't ready for me to tell my story just yet.

In 2020, it was realized I was over prescribed medication. Fibromyalgia has no cure and I was given two antidepressants and you are only supposed to take one due to the adverse complications it can trigger in your body. I became extremely ill, gained significant weight, and had absolutely no idea what was wrong until my pharmacist called me and told me what had happened. I was taking these medications for close to a year at the time it was discovered.

This led to my dark night of the soul moment. If you are not familiar, the dark night of the soul is an extremely difficult or painful period in someone's life. This all made me lose faith in western medicine and for the first time in my life, I was willing to consider anything and everything to help me heal.

I turned to spirituality. I started meditating every day. I worked with an energy healer every three days for three months to help me through this. I did evening blessings and affirmations with candles and crystals all around. I begged the universe to help me and found some breakthroughs, but I still wasn't ready yet to tell the story.

NDE (near death experience) elements are believed to include awareness of being dead in which a person experiences the world from outside the physical body may include moving through a tunnel, communication with light, observation of celestial landscape, meeting with deceased persons, life review, and more.

Fast forward three more years, I had a severe adverse reaction post-op and I had five hours of NDE elements where I saw my spirit guides, had a very high fever, and my body was fighting the wonderful treatment because it immediately went into fight mode. My body so full of distrust could not process letting go. I saw my beautiful childhood dog, Magenta, and a Native American medicine woman. Maharaja, my lion guide, let me know I was going to be okay. Once I made it through the five hours of intense fever and chills, I had a migraine for 24 hours straight. The treatment I had doesn't allow for any medication so I had to endure until my body could fight it off on its own. The feelings around shame for being so vulnerable in front of others, sobbing my heart out, things I've tried to remain hidden for so long. It was such a relief seeing everyone once I made it through and not feeling any less than. This is because I did not appreciate the human elements of life nor did I ever really want to be here for most of my life until I found a greater purpose- which is telling this story.

I always wanted to be outside my body because the core of it was so sick from years of trauma and illnesses derived from it. Several doctors and caregivers made this experience so memorable and while I don't remember a lot, I remember a sweet voice saying "you don't have to be so strong" which is what I needed to hear. I wept so very much during these five hours as I had to endure hell. I had to let go and had zero control over anything happening- something trauma survivors are not very good at. C-PTSD and fibromyalgia are trauma induced and I've had to be so strong for so long and I've carried so very much. After this experience, my higher consciousness was thriving and I finally felt peace in my own body for the first time in a long time. I've seen the most beautiful lights and colors and everything out there in the universe is beautiful.

I assure you that if you have trauma trapped in your body, you are not living life to its fullest. You are not free. My last session once I got through the worst of it was with a happiness expert who validated my decisions for cutting toxic people out of my life.

He said: "the three things all relationships should have are integrity, love, and health. If you don't have these three things, you are not choosing your happiness. We give so much to others when we don't take care of ourselves."

He then asked "would you cut your head off for me?"

I said "no way."

Then he asked "then why would you give your happiness away? It is the same thing."

When it comes to healing, it has to be everything- mind, body, and soul. Once I was fully with it again, I knew what I had to do. It was time.

Every human child deserves a childhood.

Every human being deserves respect and dignity.

So if every human being deserves those things, why do we negatively label the people who call out the ones who didn't fulfill those obligations?

Why do we celebrate the golden one, but not the black sheep?

Together, we can remember that we are worthy.

Are you ready to reclaim your story?

I'm ready to tell you mine.

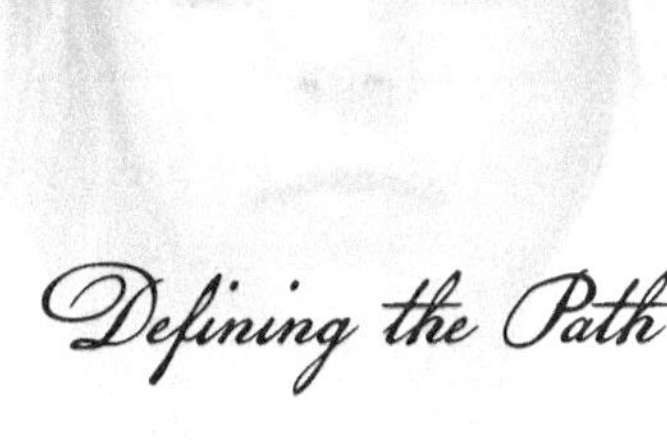

Defining the Path

Trauma- a deeply distressing or disturbing experience; a physical injury

Grief- deep sorrow, especially that caused by death or loss

Recovery- a return to a normal state of health, mind or strength; the action or process of regaining possession of or control of something that was stolen or lost

Resurgence- rising or tending to rise again; it means **coming back**

These are the four steps for the journey that lies ahead. These are the four main themes that every passage and every page will provide insights to you, inclusive of over two and half decades of writing from my life. I started journaling at a young age as it was the only outlet I truly felt comfortable talking about how I really felt. As I reread my journals, especially the oldest ones, I now recognize calls for help that I didn't know how to ask for. You will see and feel the trauma. You will see and feel the grief. And as we transition into recovery, you will still find these themes as healing is never linear. My hope for you is that when we take that final lap into resurgence, you will find ways to process those challenging parts of the journey a little bit better. There are also archetypes who were impactful to my journey in each of these different steps. They may resonate or remind you of people from yours as well- from saints to sinners, from abusers to saviors. Hold on tight, as the first step is always the hardest. I want to take you on a journey. But you have to be ready and willing. It's not a simple path. It is chaotic, with winding turns and darkness. You will be retracing footsteps on what I've endured. What I've survived. What I've overcome. This is my life. This is Worthy 2.0: The Journey of Finding HER.

This book is purposely not linear. It is written out of order, chaotic, disorganized, nightmarish, and turbulent. Streams of consciousness from my journals as a child will be shared to show how much help I truly needed, and how I mentally escaped from the abuse. This muddled path mirrors the everyday life of what it is like to function as a disabled person. It is formless and uncontrolled, to provide a day in the life of a trauma survivor and why everything is so much harder to do, even the basic little things in life. It is also written this way to show how memories at any time from our past can come to the surface and disrupt your healing. This is okay. Healing is not linear.

Let me show you the beautiful chaos of my soul.

WHAT IS WORTHY?

What is worthy? How can this word be universally defined? What deserves to be awarded or recognized?
Are you notable? Are you important? Are you special?
All human beings struggle with feelings, emotions, and life.
As people get older, they seem to care more about their legacy.
This, I guess, is if you feel like your life's work is worthy.
How can I judge that?
How can you judge me?
I know that my journey had a lot of twisted turns.
I know that my journey feels like I've been down more than I've been up.
But when you find yourself, sister, you'll be FREE.
Will you walk with me?

Down this road there is tragedy.
Down this road there is fear.
No matter how dark the day, there was always hope.
Come to me, my sister- walk with me through the trauma and the grief.
Walk with me to find the light in the darkness of recovery.
Come, be reborn with me, through our recovery and resurgence.
This path is not always straight.
Trauma can knock you down from recovery.
Grief can hold you back from resurgence.
I can't promise you a finish line as life is never certain,
but I know that we can't stay here.
So, let's go find this word together.
Let's go find "worthy."
Let's face Trauma bravely together.

Shay, 10-21-19

Trauma

“They witnessed her destruction
Then they were left to wonder why,
She saw nothing but darkness,
Though the stars shone in her eyes,
But maybe they’d forgotten,
When they failed to see the cracks,
That a star’s light shines the brightest,
When it’s starting to collapse.”
-e.h.

TRIGGERED, 2021

"We are not ourselves when we're triggered. We become who we think we need to be to SURVIVE."- Dr. Glenn Patrick Doyle

"I am not a victim."
"I am a survivor."
I say this to myself over and over as the tears well up again.
The pain in my head starts to throb a little more and the waves keep crashing over me.
The waves no one can see, but me, standing at the shoreline.

They ebb and flow in an ocean where swimmers aren't meant to swim.
They're meant to struggle keeping their heads above the water,
wondering how many more kicks they have in them before they drown.
I feel outside of my body.
My mind is gone.
Lost in a place of darkness, lost in space.
My body is lost at sea,
with a poisoned ego who punishes a broken body with the remnants of what is left of a soul.
The body, the mind, and soul are not united in this battle.
The holy trinity of being disconnected, further apart than one human lifetime should ever have to endure.
You might think- just swim to shore.
You might think- I'm not trying hard enough.
But what you don't know is my story,
How hard it is for me to even breathe, function, want to keep going, living, being,
So here I am, drowning, heart, mind, body and soul,
Broken, lost, and alone surrounded by deafening emptiness.
I'm screaming inside with words that have no meaning.
Like Demi says, "Anyone? Please send me, anyone.
Lord, is there anyone? I need someone."
This dark night of the soul was rock bottom.
Is there a chain to my ankle, weighing me down like an anchor?
Or is that just the extra baggage I carry holding me down?
I need to let go, but I don't know how.
The voice of your wounded ego says, "You deserve it."
How does one think clearly when your own mind isn't even on your team?
Your soul is nowhere to be found,
Your heart anchored on the ocean floor shattered into pieces.
As if keeping your head above water isn't hard enough,
You hear the unmistakable rumbling of thunder.
You slowly turn your head to face your greatest fear.
A royal purple thunderhead is coming your way,

gaining momentum and building, cloud upon cloud.
At this point, you're frozen in time,
Your mind recognizes the threat, but you've already endured enough.
Hard to fight when you're drowning, anchored down by the weight of pain, sorrow, trauma,
And a broken heart beneath you.
"Haven't I already done enough?"
"A lifetime of trauma and you want me to keep going?"
That ego is bruised and hurt, but snaps back into reality with danger ahead.
"Maybe I should just embrace it."
"Ride the waves, maybe I should just float along."
"If I'm meant to survive, get a second chance, maybe I'll just let go."
Elsa says to let the storm rage on, that the perfect girl is gone, facing the break of dawn.
I curl up like a cannonball, clutching my legs one last time, hugging a lifeless body,
one missing the pieces of a heart, a soul, and a mind.
Eyes are wide open as the temperature drops, the thunder roars, and the waves rage on.
Here goes nothing- embracing the unknown.
I let go of my fetal body, I'm floating along, unsure of what lies ahead.
If I may meet my end within moments, how many more breaths?
Heartbeats, memories, chances, in the moment- was I free or was I trapped?
Free from fear, or succumbing to the end?
How on earth did we get here?
"You were supposed to be THE ONE."
"The one who saves the world."
"How can you save the world when you can't even save your own damn self?"
As the waves get higher, the rain finally arrives,
lashing my face and skin above the water.
Are these raindrops or tears?
"It would be so much easier if I gave up.

Just let it all end," a voice says.
I remember my broken heart on the ocean floor,
And wonder how many of those broken pieces were of my own doing.
I wonder how many times I looked outside myself for validation and love.
Gasping for air and swallowing salt water, tears, and raindrops,
Maybe the howling wind was trying to talk to me.
There's no one else to hear your screams,
Just me, what's left of me, anyway.
Destiny, Life, Death
Why am I here?
WHY AM I HERE?
Failure, Trauma, Emptiness
WHY AM I HERE?
That next level I was scared to look at,
For I knew some of the answers.
They were housed in a very dark place.
A place I was not sure I wanted to think about again.
That voice in my head that wants to give up has to go if we're going to make it out of this.
I don't even know who is talking anymore,
But I hear, "The ego must die. Let it go. It's time to be reborn."
Destiny, Life, Death
Choices, Decisions, Realizations
The person, the voice asking in anger, was not helping the situation.
It was not serving me, my survival, and felt heavy.
"I can't see in the stormy weather.
I can't seem to hold it all together.
And I can't swim in the ocean like this forever.
And I can't breathe."
I pray that God, the universe, anyone, would rescue me,
Save me, keep my head above water.
It was time to embrace it all,
my fear, my guilt, my shame, my destiny
And if I was given a second chance,

I promised I would I would put my heart back together,
That I would find my soul,
Build a healthier mind.
Someway, somehow I would put me all back together again.
No matter what it took.
So the waves roared, the skies wept, and the winds howled,
And I was a beautiful disaster, embracing it all.
Baby girl, it's time to face the music.

THE EGO MUST DIE

"I can't do it anymore." These words echoed in my brain as I realize I am again under water. Drowning in a tub that I asked to bathe in. Self-sabotage trauma response for me again. Overcommitting, overdoing, over-existing got me again.

When the world has made you so messed up, you'll do just about anything to distract yourself to avoid doing the real work. The kind that involves looking in the mirror and facing reality. The kind where your body gives up on you and forces you to heal.

It is a delicate balance- finding purpose and peace after enduring trauma. Decades of it. You don't want to admit people with certain labels are the ones who broke you. In society, the rules say to honor them. To bow down and obey authority. This abuse must be normal if the people in charge are doing it, right?

NO.

NO NO NO.

It is your duty and obligation as a cycle breaker to end it. To stop the generational trauma and pain that is carried through the blood and bone of your ancestors. You are a dear child of the universe. It's not fair that we all carry wounds and baggage that isn't even our own. If they really loved you- really, really loved you- they wouldn't give you their baggage to carry. They would take it back, take it off your shoulders, make you feel safe and secure, and make you believe you are lovable and worthy.

It is not yours to carry, dear one.
It's not yours to bear, dear child.
It's not yours, period, little one.

What if I told you there is a way to let it all go?
What if I told you there is a path that leads you out of the darkness?
What if I told you there is a light out there for you to follow?

I understand that this is hard.
You may feel guilty, afraid, lost, and hopeless.
I've felt that way too.

It won't be easy.
This trauma may be all you've ever known.
You feel it in your bones that it is wrong, but you are afraid to escape it.

What if I told you there was another way?
That there is a place that is safe and free of it all?
What if I told you that this was a new beginning?

Maybe you're not ready yet.
It's a scary thing to set off on your own, leaving everything you've ever known behind.
I'm here to tell you my story.
I'm here to empower you to let go.
I'm here to cheer you on when you're ready.
I'm telling you my story because I know someone out there needs to hear it.
I know I'm not the only black sheep of a family.
I know I'm not the only trauma and abuse survivor.
I know I'm not the only one who has become physically sick trying to fight off the damages of being abused.
Everyone has trauma.
Mental, emotional, physical, and spiritual trauma.
None of these are easier than the other.
Some battle scars don't leave marks on our skin, but can leave bruises on our minds, breaks in our heart and fractures in our souls.
These are all layers we must protect in our humanness.

These are our own to love and protect for without them, who, and what, are we?
My wish for you is to find strength in these words.
My wish for you is to release your past.
My wish for you is to find what makes our hearts beat, our minds spin, our bodies move and our souls sing.
Come with me now, take my hand, dear one. It's time to look in the mirror and relive the trauma. It's time to face it head on. We are not dwelling on the past, we are looking for ways to be better. We are looking for ways to break the cycle. It won't be easy, but we're in this together. Every. Single. Step.
Let's take the path of Trauma's Memory Lane.

MEMORY LANE

Do you remember your first childhood memory? Was it peaceful? Joyful? Did you feel safe?

As a trauma survivor with C-PTSD, fibromyalgia, anxiety, and depression, my memories were stored under lock and key, in a cabinet somewhere in the cobwebs of my brain. It wasn't until I started inner child healing that I could even remember all of the traumatic events I endured and witnessed as a small child.

I realize now at what a young age I left my body. Complete cognitive dissonance separating my mind, my body, my spirit, and my soul.

I also realize with trauma healing being so sporadic and not linear, my memories weren't even in order anymore. A symptom of living with a disability now where everything is harder- organization, endurance, living. I even forget to breathe sometimes- holding it is a trauma response, expecting the worst out of every situation because it's all I've ever known, felt, and endured.

I can say now I was completely broken. I looked for external validation at every turn. I self-sabotaged with the best and worst of them all. I look back and all I can say to my inner child and younger self is that I'm sorry. I didn't know any better. I know better now. I now understand why I did the things I did, ultimately trying to feel better about myself. I over exercised and did not eat enough. I was anorexic for a period of time and no one stopped or helped me. I overdid it in the community, seeking validation through serving on too many boards and helping too many other people at the expense of myself. I wanted to make other people feel better to make me, myself, feel better. And I gave out all my spoons in the process. I know better now. I am sorry.

I WILL NEVER FORGET

I will never forget the day I watched the towers fall.
I watched so soundlessly that I forgot to breathe.
I will never forget the day I watched her cry.
Tears streamed down her face, as she watched the country fall apart.
I will never forget the day he laughed at us, trying to crush the American Spirit.
I will never forget the people who searched for bodies underneath the rubble of the towers with tears on their faces.
I will never forget the people who lost loved ones on a day of terror, for not just Americans, but the whole world.
I will never forget the tears I cried that day.
For the rest of my life, I will never forget.

Shay, age 12

FIBROMYALGIA

I am feeling sad today.
My back hurts.
I'm trying to work out and get back in shape, but my body isn't cooperating.
It's hard to sit eight hours a day in a chair.
It's hard to be at work all day and pretend there is nothing wrong.
This morning after my workout, I didn't really feel any endorphins.
After the accident, I lost the harmony they are supposed to give you.
Along with a peaceful mind, and joy.
Now, not only was something I love taken away from me for such a long time, but months and months of attempting various treatments- something I used to love isn't making me feel like the person I was before.
I used to be able to workout 2x/day, 5-6 days a week.
I was reaching peak performance as an athlete.
It was all taken away from me.
This isn't my fault and I shouldn't have to feel this way.
I shouldn't have to stress about money, and wonder whether or not life would be better if I wasn't here anymore.
This is not how I want to exist.
I just want it all to end.
I have not only been hurt physically, but also mentally and emotionally.
I have anxiety and depression.
I worry about paying for medical bills I should have never incurred.
I worry about never being in shape again.
I worry that I will have to live like this for the rest of my life.
I worry that I will never truly be happy again.
I'm 27 years old, and I feel so much older.
And the worst part is that no one else can feel my pain.
No one else can truly understand how I feel.

Not only do I feel pain, but I think about pain.
My mind is in pain.
I am stuck in a situation where my power and control is limited.
Sometimes a positive mindset can't fix what is broken.
This loss has broken my body, my heart, my spirit, and my mind.
Nothing is unbreakable.
They say time can heal anything, but I've been waiting and waiting to feel even just okay.
I don't need to be completely better.
And I've been trying for months and months, but everyone has a breaking point.
And I am broken.

THE NARCISSIST

"You own everything that happened to you. Tell your stories. If people wanted you to write warmly about them, they should have behaved better." - Anne Lamott

I've gone to learn at the hands of an abuser, it is hard to tell others about the abuse when it's happening.
There is shame, disappointment, and embarrassment.
I've never been so ashamed, disappointed, and embarrassed that I couldn't see past the masks sooner.
I'm ashamed that I believed that the good existed in these humans and they would stop.
I'm disappointed in myself that I didn't cut them off sooner.
And I'm embarrassed that I, of all people, am a victim.
I let myself down and I'm sorry.
Sorry for letting me accept gaslighting and believe these words:

- "You would have never gotten this without me"
- "I didn't know people who do what you do for a living got awards."
- "The only fulfillment I get from our relationship is your beauty and sweetness. You're not good for anything else."
- "I ghost those I don't love. You're lucky."
- "I'll be loyal until then. If you don't do what I want, someone else will be in my bed"
- "She doesn't need surgery. She's just doing it for attention."
- "Cancel your plans with your family or we're done"
- "You're always having a hard time with things that aren't hard"
- "You didn't do that. I had to do it because of you."
- "People who do what you do for a living are stupid. I would never ask them for help."
- "You're my person."

- "I'm tired of empty promises and that you will change and make a miraculous recovery one day"
- "If I have to ask more than once, it's disrespectful. I'm done being challenged. I'm the fucking man."
- "I'm sorry you feel I ruined your birthday."
- "I'm hotter than you now and can do better than you."

It makes me sick to think I even allowed someone who could speak such words to me in my sacred presence.

So all we can do is call them out.

How their eyes change to black when you do and they realize they've been caught.

All we can do is say "No."

All we can do is have boundaries.
All we can do is go no contact.
And when people say you're the black sheep,
It's a lonely place to be.
But nothing can be worse than living in a hell where you let people speak to you that way.
So instead you call them out.
You should be proud to be a black sheep instead of a doormat or a punching bag.
You should be proud to be alone, but know that you're not.
There are plenty of us out there cheering you on.
I know it hurts taking up space you were made to believe you didn't deserve.
Looking at these words may trigger you and I'm sorry.
I wanted you to know that this is not okay.
I wanted you to know this is not how safe people treat you.
I wanted you to know if this happens, you need to leave.
If you already did, I'm so proud.
If you're thinking about it, let this be your sign.
If you don't believe you can, it's okay.
I had to wait longer than I wanted sometimes,
But I promise you,
The right tribe is out there.
And they are nothing like this.
So call them out, black sheep, loud and proud.
It's not your job to carry broken people.
Not anymore.
I choose you, black sheep.
I choose you.

THE EVIL QUEEN

Her suitcase is packed. I tell her I don't want her to leave. I ask her to stay. Whatever words said to a small child did not make any sense. Building blocks in front of the door. Nothing I could do or say would make her change her mind. The anger and the rage of something that wasn't my fault felt heavy on my little body.

It was a scene from a bad movie. I watch her drive away. I can't sleep so I stare out of the window of my bedroom. Hoping to see headlights blind me. That it was just a bad dream. At this moment, I feel things for the first time as a child. Maybe grief? Guilt? Sadness with tears flowing.

I'm six years old and she doesn't love me.
I'm six years old and I'm not worthy of love.
I'm six years old and the only person I was taught to depend on left me.
I'm six years old and I'm scared.
I'm six years old and I don't know what to do.
I'm six years old and I don't know what tomorrow brings.
I'm six years old and I'm alone.
I'm six years old and I'm traumatized.
I'm six years old and my heart is broken for the first time.
I'm six years old and I need help.
I am six years old and I don't want to be here anymore.

Shay, Age 6

SHE IS GONE

She is gone.
She has left the world.
She will never come back.
She is gone.
Her stress bruised her heart.
Her pain broke it.
Her tears were like rivers,
Flowing endlessly.
I watched her cry.
She never stopped.
She never smiles.
Not anymore.
She is gone.
There is no more to say.
I miss her.
She is gone.

Shay, age 12

INSOMNIA

I wake up in the middle of the night thinking of all I've gone through.
Stress, fear, pain - it doesn't go away.
I think of all the things that I wished were not true.
I think of all the heroes in another part of the world.
The soldiers fighting for my freedom look endlessly for the villain,
but the villain hides from them, far beyond their reach.
It brings me hatred, thinking of the villain.
He made my country feel pain when they already had enough.
I wish the pain would go away, but it remains inside of me.
If only the pain would cease, maybe then I would sleep peacefully.

Shay, Age 12

THE WOODEN SPOON

The closet light is on in the bedroom shared with my brother. I don't know what I did. I did know there was a wooden spoon in her hand and it was going to hurt.

Once was enough. Enough to break me. Enough to make me sob hysterically. Enough to confuse me that the one with all the power intentionally hurt me. I thought her job was to protect and love me. I don't remember if there were bruises. I don't remember what happened next. I just remember the fear. The tears and sobbing flowing like a waterfall. The hopeless feeling of standing there without clothes and just taking it. I am four years old and I was just beaten for the first time. I am four years old and for the first time, I am unsure if I want to live.

Shay, Age 4

RESENTMENT

May 9th, 2006

I fight you everyday and I lose all the time.
I'm fighting something that can't be won.
It's something in your mind you can't control,
The sudden desire to be something that you'll never be.
I don't know who you are anymore,
The innocence is gone.
I've seen days of wonder,
I've seen days of fear,
Fear for your life and what you will become.
Although my existence has no importance
In that cold heart of yours,
I will wait for the day that time no longer matters,
and the surroundings around you don't matter,
because in the end the only thing that does matter is your tribe.
Your family, your friends,
How's your family looking?
How are your relationships?
Who even cares about you?
Because one day all the things you hide,
will be found out by the ones you "love",
and those who surround you will slowly disappear.
And all the bad choices that you made,
will follow you like a shadow that never goes away.
And I'll be watching.
That's for damn sure.

HELP

May 10th, 2006

Today was another regular day.
She spoke to me as if she knew who I was,
But she'll never know who I really am.
I've always wondered if it would come to this,
A drifting departure that is no longer able to come back for the final time.
If love of another could steer you,
through the day without fear or complaints,
who could imagine something so simple or so stupid,
That life could make someone so miserable.
Help seems too far away,
I need your help,
but it's not something you're capable of,
and my patience is growing thin.
This may be the final time I ever stand up for you,
because when I finally watch you fall,
I might not help you get up again,
and you should completely understand.

PRETEND

I hope you find yourself out there in the world where you can get so easily lost.
Through the fire, the fog, and the wind, you must brave it all.
I can't pretend anymore that I mean these smiles.
I cannot waste any extra effort pretending I'm okay when I'm not.
This new world of where you're supposed to pretend you have it all together,
Well I don't because the voices aren't cheering anymore,
They're saying words I never thought they would,
Like Amy Lee screams, "I want to die."
I understand the thinking of how you want to go,
Whether by flight or height, I would rather just sleep forever than wake up to this again.
Is it really so bad to wish it would just all go away?

CHILD SOLDIER

Like Jesus carried his cross, the soldiers have carried Lady Liberty for our nation,
Such heavy burdens to carry for God, our country and for all of creation,
And yet, you expected me to carry you.
Ever since I was a child and you took me to church and made me believe,
Ever since 9/11 when the buildings were falling,
I didn't understand and all you did was cry on your sleeve,
And you made me carry you.
Jesus never stopped your anger, the packing of your suitcase,
You threatened to leave us so many times in time and space,
And you made me carry you.
Sometimes I would build blocks in front of the door praying,
I was more afraid you would leave and never come home, maybe more of you staying.
I didn't know any better the difference between love and hate,
and you made me carry you.
I was afraid of the darkness within you so I tried to be perfect in every way so you never got mad,
But I was never perfect, never good enough for it to stay within, and remember only being sad.
Maybe it wasn't me today, or my brother or sister,
But if it was any one of us we all suffered together like a ritualistic twister,
The twisters destroyed the meaning of a family home,
and you made us all carry you.
Being away from home was safer than going home and seeing what kind of mood you were in each day,
You were never on our team, we didn't know what to say,
and we had to carry you.
Was there ever a Holiday you felt that we did well enough?
It never felt that way, it never felt enough.
I was never enough,
and you expected me to carry you.

With darkness as black as the night, what was good left in your soul became harder to find,
I tried so hard to believe it was still there, but over time I started losing mine,
And yet you expected me to carry what was left of yours.
You made a child feel inadequate at the expense of feeling a little more great,
As if something so cruel could fix a lifetime of insecurity and self-hate,
And you expected me to carry you.
Even if I was drowning or unable to keep up the pace,
You probably wouldn't notice because all you could see is you winning this race,

And you expected me to carry you.
Head under water, I can no longer lift you high,
For if I never let go, you would probably let me die,
And you expected me to carry you still.
So I let go and you lose control, you lose your mind and say I'll be the one to blame,
As if a child is not allowed to make any play calls in this game,
And you expected me to let you win.
This is my life and I can't carry you anymore,
You disown me and lie to everyone as if I was some stupid little whore,
And you expected me to give in and pick you up again.
You call me names, you tell your lies, you do nothing but overreact,
Suddenly fake news and lies mustard gas all the facts,
And you expected me to come back to you.
You send me things as if you can buy me back,
But I'm a human with feelings and emotions, it doesn't work like that,
And you expected me to let it go.
Months turn into years, you never once were looking in the mirror,
to see how your darkness has ruined every meadow, every flower,
Instead you blame your children for flaws and failings and expect forgiveness because you are in power.
I'm an adult now, and I won't carry you,
I won't kneel to you,
I won't ever give in again.
My life is better without your reign of terror and I have broken the chain.
Any power, any control no longer exists.
Your darkness is only the bane of your existence.
I cannot fix what is broken, only you can,
But you don't want to, so let me say it again:
Your weight is too heavy for my light and my soul,
Your darkness only clouds my life and goals,
And you expect me to leave a place for you.
The darkness will never heal if you don't want it to,

and now we must all carry a bit of your evil inside of us that you melted through,
For the scars of your pain will never go away,
You broke our hearts each and every day.
Broken children with broken hearts that must soldier on,
You are no longer welcome here and are the one that must move on.
Respect and boundaries, things as children we never learned,
Until it was too late to realize you had no idea what they were or how they were earned.
You can carry that forever, our pain and our scars,
If you had some too, it's too late to understand what they are.
For a parent should never say "If you think I'm bad, you have no clue",
Children shouldn't be threatened just because you feel we are one to you.
The house we grew up in was never a home,
Please leave us to our trauma and leave us alone.
For there is nothing left for any of us to say,
Except I can't carry you and should have never had to, have a nice day.
Jesus, the soldiers, the fighters,
A child soldier, another kind of martyr.
For a lifetime of trauma to deal with through our lives,
We must band together, my brothers and sisters, to survive.
Everyone's cross is valid that we carry everyday.
Do not allow anyone else to make you feel any other way.
Hold my hand, walk with me, we must leave this behind,
What is done is done and we must respect our time.
Go live, hold your head high and breathe,
For maybe the greatest thing we do is move on and just be.

HYPERVIGILANCE

Is the closet closed enough so the monsters can't come out at night?
Is the blanket covering all my toes so they don't grab me and pull me under?
Are the doors locked?
Where are my keys?
Am I ever safe?
Afraid to get gas at a gas station.
Afraid to drive on the interstate so we take the back roads.
Afraid to leave the house after dark.
Afraid to walk down the street without checking behind.
Am I ever safe?
Try to let go but your mind can't.
Try to breathe normally but your body can't.
Try to sleep but you're afraid of the monsters.
Try to move but your body is in shock from just a trigger.
Just a trigger.
Am I ever safe?
Act perfect so you don't get in trouble.
Please don't yell at me, I'm trying my best.
Speak politely and say you're good.
Please don't ask invasive questions, I can't say anymore.
Keep your head down so they don't see the tears in your eyes.
Please just leave me alone- I'm fine.
It's a door slamming.
It's a suitcase by the door.
It's someone raising their voice.
It's the fear of disappointment.
It's the inability to be perfect.
It's the fear of being left behind.
It's the fear of never being loved.
Am I ever safe?
Just because it wasn't intentional doesn't mean it won't trigger me.

Just because you don't think it was so bad doesn't mean my nervous system feels the same way.
Just because you think your behavior is normal doesn't mean you're not responsible for what you've done to me.
Just because you think you had it worse doesn't mean I deserve this.
Actions speak louder than words they say, but how could words do this to me?
Maybe it was more than that.
It was the fear that sucked the life out of my body every time your bedroom door opened.
It was holding my breath waiting to see if I was in the clear or not-for at least a moment.
It was the flight mode activated where I left my body so I didn't have to be present, at least in my mind.
I never want to lose control of myself again.
Am I ever safe?
But I lost control over my heart rate because every time I'm afraid, it elevates.
My palms sweat.
I forget how to breathe again.
This perfectionism trauma response where I feel like no one will love or value me,
Because you made me feel like I was nothing.
I'm afraid to say anything at all or admit that I was human.
What if they leave me like you?
What if they pack their suitcase and leave me like you?
Am I ever safe?
Oh, so you want me to clap for you?
Because you came back?
Does that make this all better?
You had it worse, so that erases your actions somehow?
You don't get to decide how I feel.
YOU DID THIS TO ME.
Flowers bloom in gardens where they are nurtured, but I'm not a fucking flower.

I'm a goddamn tree with my roots in the earth.
I stand tall, not for you, but for HER.
Storms come, but I do not waver.
Not anymore.
I am safe.
I accept my triggers, for they were just trying to protect the little scared girl inside.
I accept my trauma, for it has made me who I am.
I accept my scars, for they remind me of how far I've come and the battles I've fought.
I accept my condition, for this was all just part of the plan.
I'm never going back again.
I am safe.
Today the closet door is slightly open but I am not afraid.
The blanket may not fully cover my feet.
The gas station is not so scary.
The world holds space for someone like me.
The world is accepting of someone like me.
Stand in your truth.
Speak your power.
You don't live there anymore.
This is all you've ever needed to believe, dear one.
We are safe.
The triggers will still come.
They don't define you.
I've come this far.
The monsters are still out there,
But I don't carry them anymore.
For I built my own house.
And I make the rules now.
I am safe.
My body still tenses up.
My mind still looks for danger.
My heart still doesn't like my back to a door.
My soul is exhausted from all the running.

My palms still sweat.
My heart rate still climbs.
I'm just so tired,
But I am safe.
Hypervigilant.
Fibromyalgia.
C-PTSD.
Migraines.
Nausea.
IBS.
This is how my body tries to fight you, and the body keeps the score.
But I am safe now.
I don't know what deficit I started at.
I don't know how many times I started over again.
I don't know how many times I cried.
I don't know how many times I was triggered.
I should have fought back.
I should have stood up for myself.
I should have been there for HER.

But I'm here now,
And we are safe.
My biggest regret will never be letting you go.
My biggest regret will always be failing HER.
Over and over.
But it's equitable to the amount of times you let her down, over and over.
And for some reason, you still think you deserve access to the empire I built.
For some reason, in spite of all this, you still think I'm your property.
But those chains broke a long time ago.
I am safe now.
It was the moment you decided to make me the villain.
It was the moment you twisted my words.
It was the moment you turned us all against each other.
Hurt people hurt people.
But I wasn't just anyone.
I was your favorite.
Until I asked for what I deserved,
And now I am the safe one.
But first, I was the black sheep.
Then I was the one who made you look in the mirror.
And you didn't like what you saw.
And you didn't like accountability.
And then I went from gold to black.
Ashes to ashes- we all fall down.
But what you didn't realize was who you were fucking with.
I am safe.
Burn me down, I rise up.
I am a Phoenix, after all.
And I will burn to protect this house over and over and over again.
HER and I are safe, forevermore.

AFRAID

October 15th, 2019

Being able to speak and being able to communicate are two very different things.

The answers I could create as a child were short and straight to the point.

Words like "I'm fine" or "I'm good" or "I'm okay."

That's what other people and kids said, so I thought that was what I was supposed to say.

Anything beyond that seemed to lead conversations that were uncomfortable.

It was safer saying less than more- so that's what I did.

I was afraid.

I was afraid to get into trouble, to get yelled at, always afraid of the reactions.

I was so afraid that instead of being honest, I decided to be as perfect as possible.

So that way words like "I'm fine" or "I'm okay" were believed.

I tried to explain it to a couple of friends over the years and felt safest in their homes.

There at least there was love.

The only place as a child I felt truly safe to use my voice was with my pen and my journal.

My words were dark and sad, but it wasn't until I was much older that I would understand why.

I couldn't write about happy things or healthy relationships or love because I didn't know what they were.

You can't love someone without trust.

Most importantly, you can't love someone if you can't openly and honestly communicate with them or vice versa.

These are the foundations of any healthy relationship.

We all make mistakes.

We are all human, but if you can't meet these minimum requirements…I don't know.

I've let too many people walk over me because I was afraid to use my voice.

You didn't show me how.

I was afraid to tell people "no".

I was afraid to stand up for myself.

I was afraid of you because you made me afraid of you.

You ruled with fear and the only person's feelings who mattered were yours.

My feelings were made to be nothing so I felt like I was nothing.

There was no respect and no trust.

You would go throw my trash, looking for God knows what.

I was so afraid- I was this angel on the outside, but inside I was nothing.

Just a scared little girl, trying to breathe to stay alive.

My trauma response was something I felt I could never overcome.

I did try when I was older to put boundaries in place where I could feel empowered.

And when I was brave enough to speak up, you didn't trust, respect, or communicate in a healthy manner.

You verbally destroyed me as a person, what I do for a living, my achievements, everything YOU should be proud of.

So no, you don't get to keep gaslighting me with your poisonous words and empty promises.

You don't get to tell me who I am and what to do.

Not anymore.

So I will tell my story in hopes that one day, you will tell yours too.

Maybe you don't say it out loud, maybe you'll just write it down.

Maybe there's no one you trust,

But you can trust me.

I'll never know your pain, but it is valid for my sisters and brothers.

Most importantly, you are WORTHY.

YOU ARE WORTHY.

It's time to move on and let this go.

Here's my hand.

It might not always be easy.
There might be more pain to come, but at least we will be free.
Take a deep breath.
Grab my hand.
One step at a time.
One day at a time.
Together, my sister, my brother,
We are FREE.

JUST BREATHE

Sometimes I forget to breathe.
Most of life is just breathing through each moment to move to the next.
I held my breath so much as a child because there was so much uncertainty.
Each moment questioning how to move to the next when you're frozen.
So much has been trapped around my heart.
And now the trauma lives in my chest,
The bones, the ligaments, the joints,
The muscles, the tissues, the fascia.
Whoever said trauma can't live in the body
Never read "The Body Keeps the Score"
And I've been living in a deficit for so long,
I don't even know how long it will take me to reach zero.
How do I stop myself from falling down further?
How do I tell myself I can't live here anymore?
There is no comfort staying in the same space here.
Especially when I already can't breathe.

IN MOURNING

It's time to move on from this trauma and let this go. It might not always be easy. There might be more pain to come, but at least you'll be free in your grief. Together, we can mourn the loss of you, the former version of yourself. We can't be that person anymore. So take a deep breath, grab my hand. One step at a time, we move onto the next level of our grief.

Grief

"Grief, I've learned, is really just love. It's all the love you want to give, but cannot. All that unspent love gathers up in the corners of your eyes, the lump in your throat, and in that hollow part of your chest. Grief is just love with no place to go." - Jamie Anderson

GONE

The mercy is gone.
It died in the mother's arms, bleeding like a river that never ceases.
The peace is gone.
It disappeared like a kidnapped child,
Searching for the answer, but never seen again.
The hope is gone.
It faded like a sunset, failing to rise again.

Sending the world into darkness.
The love is gone.
It broke into pieces like a broken heart.
Deserted like a troubled child.

Reaching for something to hold onto.
The life is gone.
It breathed in its last breath.
Shivering as all light leaves the world,
And a cloud of darkness overtakes all.

Shay, 2004

EPIC FAILURE, 2008

When I fall or fail, I completely lose everything I stand for, but nobody feels it as badly or as much pain as I do.
When you see it through your own eyes, it makes the pain so much worse.
It makes the disappointment elevated to a pressure point, and I fall even harder.
Things can't have a new beginning, no matter how hard you try to put it on track.
It always finds a way to stray from the finish line.
That's the problem with all of this …
I've fought epic battles that have ended in epic failure, but also found myself through glorious victories.
I've grown in wisdom with the knowledge of there will always be somebody better, stronger, faster, smarter,
so I must engineer everything to become something more,
To find an edge, a chance, to lift myself to another level.
I am someone that has changed throughout space and time and has found something more than I ever thought I had.
I thought I might never be anything greater than what others expected of me.
I brought myself down mentally, doubted myself physically, had no faith in the person who mattered most- me.
I have walked down many paths, straying, falling, lost and confused,
Where every emotion of anger and frustration followed my steps.
But here I am, with you by my side.
I wish you could feel how tired and exhausted and frustrated I am, for not achieving a level higher than the mountain top.
To have the greatest fear of being common, to be like everybody else.
I wanted the world inside my hands, to be grasped in my reach,
To sit calmly and patiently as I become everything I wanted, but I found the world will be bigger than I'll ever be.
Harder to become something in a world where being the greatest is not measured by your character,

but land, and money, and things only those with luck or fortune seem to possess.
I wish to possess something that no one could ever achieve,
No one could surpass, destroy me, break me into pieces,
To reach this level of achievement and glory that people can only dream of.
But I lack so much.
I'm afraid of so much.
Must there be so much to everything in this life, everything that I am.
I'm sorry I failed you.
It is something I'll have to live with the rest of my days, and I don't know if I can be forgiven.
So many aspirations, dreams, beliefs-I do believe,
but I'm beginning to realize that everything I could ever want to achieve.
The past haunts me with each step of victory or defeat.
I regret, and hurt, and ache from the pains and the injuries of the past,
the present is difficult for me to endure,
and the future is the only thing I can look forward to.
I'm so close and yet so far from where I should be- the finish line.
Can someone recover from losing such a feat?
I am trying to find my way to where I belong,
but no one really knows where that is.
I can only better myself, attempt to fix what flaws I have,
but I am nothing without you believing in me.
I've been so low, so close to the breaking point,
I've been broken, but you've tried to fix me.
It hurts to know that crying never fixes anything.
It is temporary relief from unbearable disappointment and pain.
I really need you to know, that it was not my intention to become this,
For I am strong, but should be so much more.
I am tough, but not tough enough.
The misery of failure is like the living dead,
You walk and talk but you are nothing,
just flesh with no soul, no mind,
nothing but the greatest waste of time and space,
that has ever walked this earth.

FREEDOM

I think I hit the plateau, running up a hill and falling backwards so many times I've lost count.
Not that I could keep track anyway with the fog that clouds my mind.
A broken body from the falling, a broken soul from the defeats.
How many times must I fall and lose before this sick cycle ends?
I thought for a long time that being strong and positive could make this easier,
Instead positivity can be toxic too.
Not everyone can get back up when they fall down.
Not everyone gets a chance to conquer all the adversity thrown their way.
This isn't to say that trying again is hopeless.
This is to say I understand that the darkness sometimes wins.
When the choice is between daily misery, I understand that you don't want to end your life, you just want the pain to stop.
So now I say from a place of great darkness,
I wish to fall asleep and never wake up in this body again.
No pain, no sadness before I go.
Just freedom from a life that I can no longer conquer.

WORTHLESS

And here it comes again,
Always the slow burn.
The fiery ripples start again,
Wrapping their ugly swirls around my arms, wrists, and hands.
I slept eight hours, and yet, I still can't move.
The fatigue from the burning is too much.
Sometimes I don't know if I'm sick because I feel like I have a fever but I don't.
It's just the power of the fire within.
Sometimes I sweat through my clothes and it's embarrassing.
Will my torso and legs catch fire too?
Will this last a few hours? A few days? A few weeks?
Only time will tell.
How did we get here?
What did I do to deserve this?
Why me?
Easy questions that seem to flip the switch of victim mode.
That's what they say- always blaming others instead of looking in the mirror,
But the reality is the abuser blames the victim for speaking up every damn time.
There's not much you can do when laying in bed wishing you were healthy.
That you had meaning or purpose.
That others believed that too, despite being unable to keep up.
They stopped inviting me.
They stopped including me.
They stopped acknowledging me.
While when you see them in passing and they act concerned,
They weren't there when it mattered.
They made you feel alone and worthless when you already felt that way.

So here I am again, remembering all the times I had no one there except a dog or two.
Here I am burning, trying to decide if any of this is worth it.
The intrusive thoughts come back.
No one was there for you.
No one could love you.
They'll just leave like she did.
You'll never be in shape again.
You're lazy.
You're worthless.
All I can do is sit with this.
Remember the day after it passes.
That I've risen up more times than fallen in this life.
This is who I am.
They can't see the flames.
They don't understand.
They never will.
But that doesn't mean I am the things my mind tells me when it's triggered.
That doesn't mean that my matter doesn't matter.
I take up space in this world, differently abled, but abled.
There has to be a reason behind the flames.
In a world where we don't always consider the everyday struggles of one another, consider this:
My invisible illness means I have fewer spoons than you.
You start with 10, I start with 6-8.
We don't discard the spoons the same way.
I wake up counting how many I have and consider what has to be done today.
You wake up without even thinking about it.
Anger, resentment, grief.
I am allowed to be angry.
I am allowed to be resentful.
I am allowed to grieve.
I thank those feelings for being human.

And reminding me that it's okay to live there, I just can't stay there.
I have to believe there is more to this.
I have to believe there is more to me.
So I lie here, wishing for more than just existing, surrounded by invisible flames with an invisible illness, and wonder:
Am I invisible too?
I'm tired of posting these photos which lead the world to believe I exist with beautiful skin and hair.

That photo doesn't represent me anymore.
I am a fighter.
I will not exist only to survive.
I will not exist to suffer.
I will exist and tell my story.
I will not rest until then.
People are drawn to beauty, not the reality of pain.
I want to paint a picture that shows you the real me.
The one who doesn't always have enough spoons to get through the day.
The one who can't get out of bed sometimes.
When I look at her I think- my god, how beautiful.
When I lie in bed thinking about how much I hate all of this I think- my god, how fake.
People often speak of the complexities of life.
The wide range of emotions that go along with it.
Well, I only ever lied if I was afraid to get into trouble.
Are you going to blame me for painting a picture that all of this is an invalid representation of life?
That I hope to break your social media down to tell us a real story?
That I want to see how human you really are?
No one ever wants to hear the journey.
How the days were long, and the nights were too.
No one wants to tell you growing up and living is fucking hard.
And then on top of all of this, people are carrying buckets filled with water.
Mine is fibromyalgia.
Mine is C-PTSD.
Mine is anxiety that comes back in moments I'm triggered.
My friends, I am not beautiful.
But, my story is.
And I won't lie.
So I will find comfort in my routine.
Breathe.
Lie on my sofa with my weighted blanket.

Snuggle my puppy.
Taking up space, just like you.
Order food for when I don't have a spoon to give.
And I believe I will survive another day.
I will survive another day to tell the tale.

PAIN SCALE

There are different levels of pain just like there are different levels of sickness.

When people ask, on a scale of 1-10, how would you rate your pain, what are we comparing it to? We may not have yet experienced the worst pain of our lives yet, and don't know what a ten really feels like, and I hope you never do?

How do you weigh sickness? By how heavy the day feels? How bad your heart hurts from pushing on, despite it being so broken? The greatest level of pain and sickness cannot be defined by a limit; it has no boundaries. The pain and sickness can be overcome if we just remember to keep breathing. Nothing is permanent, yet the chronic flaring in my arms says otherwise. It may never go away, but neither does my willingness to go on, despite the voices in my head screaming at me.

THE COURT JESTER

Adult: a person who is fully grown or developed
Happy birthday to the man who hung me out to dry.

You let me be crucified while telling others you agreed with me.
I knew it was out of my hands so I turned to you.
I tried to warn you because you said you were going to try to help, but never did.
I called you because I'm the child, and sick of being the only adult in the room.
You never asked why I called.

I NEEDED YOUR HELP.
So no, I'm not going to answer your phone calls.
You betrayed me.
You betrayed all of us.
It wasn't actually the treatment that I endured that solidified this decision for me.
It was the stories the others told me that did.
This game is disgusting and I'm disgusted that you aren't treating us fairly and equally.
I'm not playing anymore.
My life is better without the stress and drama of all this ridiculous nonsense.
I feel like I'm in middle school and won't be treated like this.
I'm the youngest, yet I seem to be the only one with gumption.
Thanks for the invite to your party that you invited me to only out of shame.
Get her help and leave me alone.
Peace and healing for me does not include you.
I sure don't like adulting,
But at least I do it.

ALONE

Leave me alone in my dungeon of despair
None now care of my existence, I am nothing
Nothing in this cruel, blackened world
I expect no love from the lies of my pain
Leave me in my shadows
For none now could be seen
Of my scarred and ugly face
That beauty knows no more
I hide behind the emptiness
That envelops my mind
I've given all I've ever had
Leave me now alone.

Shay, 13 years old

PRIVILEGE

People talk a lot about privilege and whatever they wish they had. A truly able body would be that for me, but also a mind free from the trauma and triggers. Mental and physical health are so deeply tied together- you cannot have one without the other. When everyday life is filled with triggers that make you want to fight or flight, or disassociate from your body even though you've freed yourself from the danger of your past, it is really disheartening.

It is a harmful narrative when people don't believe you as well.

Most people come from households where their children are the center of their universe. My life taught me survival mode, and I have been trying to teach my nervous system and mind how to believe I am safe my entire life. My earliest childhood memory is disturbing and there isn't much else there that I can go back in time and tell people about. I learned to disassociate myself from my body at such a young age, which makes learning to be present so hard. If you can wake up every day feeling safe, proud of yourself, and loved without fear- this is truly the greatest blessing of all.

Psychological safety is the ultimate privilege to me.

Shay, age 32

Grief

Look at me
I'm dying
Dying from exhaustion of you
Using me, showing me something I don't need to see
Lying to me like it does not matter
Leaving me alone in the dark
With no shelter and no love.
I have no more to prove
Don't look at me
Leave me alone if I'm no good to you anymore
Like a used teddy bear.
I guess I've served my purpose
No more good, just collecting dust
Like all those you've used before.
Don't look at me
Go Away
To your own little world that matters so much
So much more than me
I can't count on someone who isn't there
I thought I made a bond
But I really made a web
A web that branches off
Leaving me to be the spider who crawls over those whom you branch onto.
A loner.
A loner with no purpose.
I need something
Something to know I exist
In my world that doesn't matter to you.

I do have a purpose
Twisted in the hands of fate
I watch and wait for the signs
For me to move on and prove to the world why God put me here.
Help me.
I'm desperate for support
Obstacles are many and confidence is few
Little things are more important than you know
Which are my problems
Problems to block my purpose
I love you more than you know
So that you choose to ignore it
Like the little things
Such as me.

OUR ANGEL FROM ABOVE

A loving soul has passed away.
She has gone to a better place.
Away from fear, away from pain.
Taken into God's grace.

A legacy of love she has left behind,
So we can cherish what now remains,
But now she lives with us in spirit,
And lives without any pain.

Tears of pain should not be shed,
Tears of joy should instead

Remember her words of wisdom
Remember the life she led.

Gracious and understanding,
Gentle and full of love.
Will now always be remembered
As our angel from above.

Shay, age 13

I'M NOT SORRY

Stars glitter in the sky, moon shining in a velvet dress.
It wraps its arms around me, sheltering my eyes from the light.
What a coincidence, no light to shine a path.
My tears are hidden from the master of the sky.
Tears I cry are gone, they're gone forever.
No more tears for you, no more sense of caring.
You've wasted my time, now I waste your tears.
I'm not sorry, not sorry,
For you deserve to suffer.
Suffer like I have before, make you feel my pain.
Deserted I will make you,
I will you to reach the end.
You cut me down.
You broke me into pieces.
You have no time, time to meet your end.
I want you to be gone, gone forever.
Never to be seen again.
Gone like an apparition, leaving me to reach my dreams.
You have no purpose, you have no wisdom.
You shattered my dreams- dreams I wanted so bad.
I want you to disappear, never to show your face.
Gone so I can live, leave me so I can sleep.
Go away, go away.
You have no meaning.
You need to find something in your mind that's real.

Shay, 2004

FORGIVE ME

May 22nd, 2006

Forgive me.
I forgot once again what I was trying to do.
I was distracted from all the pain inside my very soul.
I was laughed at and mocked at by those who once stood beside me.
I carelessly left you on a hill when I should have stood right there beside you.
I'm sorry.
I could not keep up the pace,
It seems I never can,
Or ever will,
And no matter how hard I try,
It seems I'm following a dot in the distance.
Why is it so easy for you and not for me?
Forgive me.
I know you think I'm slacking,
But my legs are screaming and I can't go on anymore.
No breaths can handle my broken body,
I've lost all sense of thought and fight how I long to be like them.
I'm sorry.
Forgive me.

FOR ALL THINGS

A pitiful soul searches alone for something that doesn't seem to exist,
Searching everyday, endlessly, for that someone.
Lost in the dark, dismal world full of disaster,
Empty and barren the once fruitful plains,
That now are so lonely like her soul.
Why can't she find her love she searches for endlessly?
Loneliness clouds her eyes, just like the river of tears,
Desperate tears that fall like rain.
Pleading with the Maker for her life,
Hours pass like days, days pass like years.
'Til finally the day comes when she can take no more.
Poor Juliet falls down the endless staircase without ever knowing where Romeo went.
Tragedy is no longer a myth, but an innate part of life,
For all things begin and end without purpose.

Shay, 2004

DIFFICULT

June 3rd, 2006

Who could ever believe that my life could become so complicated?
I'm confused and disoriented.
I don't know–who to trust, who to believe,
Or who to call my friends.
Who could ever imagine such a chaotic mess?
I don't know.
I just don't know who to follow, or should I lead?
And where should I go?
I just don't understand.
Why is this so difficult for someone like me?

ENOUGH DAMAGE

October 16th, 2019

And yet the villains of the story don't seem to understand that my silence does not stem directly from my trauma, but the even deeper trauma of people, my blood, and my best friends. It is unforgivable to take on the biggest and hardest job in the world, having and raising children, and then to not love all your children. In toxic situations like these, you must learn to be okay with people not knowing your side of the story. Even for the do-gooders and the righteous at heart, you don't have anything to prove to anyone. In your silence, toxic people will try to blame you for the reaction you have without ever addressing their actions. When you try to build boundaries, hold firmly on, for they will continue to attack you. They will keep coming back, but you have to ignore their words. They may say things like "I'm sorry you feel"—but they're never sorry. They only want the control and power they had over you back.

If this started as a child, you may not understand that this is not normal behavior, since this is coming from an adult who you believe loves you and has your best interests in mind. The more and more it happens, the more and more normal it becomes to you. Without realizing it, each time it does happen, the smaller and smaller you become, as if pieces of your heart are breaking. By the time you understand trust, respect and what healthy communication and relationships are, the weight of the mistreatment and trauma are so heavy, you doubt the ability to repair yourself.

There isn't just grief of losing pieces that you try to gather and glue back together. There is the grief of living a lie for years and years because that's what you had to do to survive. It is not easy running away or breaking the power and control they had over you, but you'll never find yourself if you never walk out the door. You may think you need them, but you don't. You don't need anyone who hurts you, lies to you, gaslights, or abuses you. They've already done enough damage.

You need you. You need to find the pieces they broke. You need to walk away, or you will never find the peace you deserve. It will be one of the hardest things you ever do- saying goodbye in silence. There will be tears and there will be heartache. But there will also be peace when you take the power and the control back. You deserve to be free. The first step will be the hardest, but then you'll find your wings and fly away from a past that does not define you anymore. You can't be blamed for things you weren't controlling. Now you are free to make decisions and be happy, because the weight of the world is off your shoulders. Once you take flight, there's no looking back.

They say when you are a child, you want to be a hero like Superman or Wonder Woman. When you're an adult, you can understand villains. Well, I will never understand a villain treating a child poorly. Children are innocent until someone takes that away. Just because you were treated poorly as a child will never justify continuing the vicious cycle. As an adult, you are responsible for breaking the cycle because that's the right thing to do. That is the kind of hero children deserve. Be the hero and break the cycle before your child believes you were the villain all along.

I NEED

I need to know if you're up there.
I need to know if you're watching over me.
I need to know if you're the one giving me that extra edge.
I need to know if you're the one helping me survive the day.
I need to know if you're waiting for me at the Gates.
I need to know if you exist so I can believe again.
I need to believe more but doubts and questions confuse me so much.
I need to know you're giving me the words that I write.
I need to know that you're watching over me everyday.
I need you to know that I need you,
So that I can believe that you need me.

Shay, age 14

YOU HAD TO STAY

You had to stay.
Nowhere else was home.
Nowhere else was safe.
They made you believe the world was evil.
They made you believe they were the knights in shining armor.
They made you believe you had it good.
They made you believe it was all normal.
But it was never normal.
And you don't realize it until you're old enough to understand.
And you don't realize what a circus it all was.
And you don't realize that abuse isn't just physical pain.
And you don't realize that you were depressed and sick all the time because of them.
And yet, you had to stay.
No one believes you unless there are bruises.
No one believes you unless you have the threats in writing.
No one believes that a person in power would hurt a child.
No one believes a child without bruises.
And you don't realize the trauma that a child has.
And you don't realize the sickness festers inside.
And you don't realize the dark clouds it forms above the child's head.
And you don't realize how normal is no longer normal for that child ever in their life.
No one cheers for the child that is the black sheep.
No one cheers for the person who says they cut off their family.
No one cheers for the adult child who calls out toxic behavior to the people in power.
No one stands behind them unless they understand.
But I do.
I really fucking do.

DISASSOCIATION

So if I asked you what's the worst thing that has ever happened to you, do you even have to stop and think?
Do you automatically know it off the top of your head?
See, that's where we are different.
For if you asked me, I would tell you that I don't know.
For I'm not sure what the measurement scale is to help me decide.
Is it physical or emotional abuse?
Can you see the scar, or is it hidden under a fake smile?
Perhaps that is the tragedy in itself- you know, and I don't even know where to start.
And I'm not saying I had it worse than anyone else,
I'm just saying my brain is still processing all that encompasses being alive on this planet.
For there wasn't time to stop and pause and reflect on all of the moments where my brain left my body.
Where my mind stopped recording so it wouldn't have to remember.
But now that I've healed more, I remember more of the good days,
Walking on the beach, catching beads at a parade, and singing Love Shack in the living room,
Why couldn't that little girl just live there in those moments she felt alive?
These are questions I can't be stuck in anymore.
For that little girl still lives in me,
And we can walk on the beach together,
We can go find ways to reclaim those moments,
We can sing again like before we became so afraid to tell the world who we really are.
So if I asked the question again, what's the worst thing that has ever happened to me,
I would say for not healing sooner for HER so she could have started to remember the good a little bit more than the day before.
But now we can celebrate, look at the past with gratitude, and honor the journey of how we found ourselves.

We can build a new timeline where we honor the new version of HER as we take more steps towards self-actualization.
Whether a mountain to climb or a pyramid, all I ever wanted was to stand at the top holding HER hand and finally being able to sing again.
The joy and the happiness of that moment is what I live for.
For I cannot rest until then.
I'm coming, dear one.
I'm coming.

RUNNING, CRAWLING, WALKING

Thirty years into this life and I wonder if we all really find the purpose needed to make it far enough to find fulfillment. I have a wonderful group of friends and support, but I feel like I'm alone often. Not because no one is there; rather, no one else endures and feels the pain and pressure I am under. When I was eleven years old, my life changed dramatically. I grew up in a matter of seconds, but was so afraid of speaking up about why I was the way I was. No one knew what was really going on because I was kind and quiet. No one knew how controlled I was and how depressed I was because I kept my head down pretending like everything was fine. It wasn't until I was 25 that I realized that the people who said they loved me the most were my biggest burdens. It wasn't until I was 27 that I said enough was enough. Now that I'm 30 and understand mental illness and healthy relationships and communication, I realize I've learned from seeing the worst. I know what respect and being a friend really means. I am free from this now, yet feel so heavy walking around because the past destroyed so much for me. It is hard to move on.

Somedays, I think it won't matter what I accomplish next or the next great thing to come my way because I am still so hurt and depressed, realizing how corrupt love can really be. I didn't deserve this, and yet, I have to carry on and try to keep my head above water. The trauma has left scars on my body so deep, I see them every day and think I've come so far only to feel more and more like I am nothing. Standards and goals are limitless because of the pain of yesterday and the trauma I live with today that may last forever. Chronic pain and disease flares within me, all because the ones who were supposed to never really loved me.

I was just a pretty prize that was possessed by a demon for too long. My body and my soul crave freedom. A lonely path ahead leaving behind this baggage. I can't breathe carrying this cross anymore.

Every time I let go, it lingers like a shadow that won't leave me alone. Where can I find peace? Where can I find comfort? I never want to feel like this again in this life or the next. A goodbye should be a wall, yet they keep breaking down walls and crawling over them time and time again. How much further do I have to go to leave this all behind? A broken body can only make it so far. I fear it will never end. So I keep running, crawling and walking until I can't anymore.

THREE KINDS OF LOSSES

I suppose I was lucky that I was 30 before I lost anyone close to me. Funny how it changes your view on mortality and shows how fragile we all are. When I was a little girl, I was convinced that one day things would get better and easier because nothing could be as bad as the present. I thought the struggle and pain would feed a never ending fire of fixing all the time I had lost already. Instead, it seems the next mountain to climb is ready as soon as you climb the one before. A never ending cycle of pain and grief with a sprinkle of joy and few people you love.

I've seen three kinds of losses: the loss of a loved one, the loss of a living loved one, and loss of a former version of yourself. All three hurt, but make sure you never lose yourself.

THE WALL, 2007

The wall is see-through, yet firm and formidable.
It is unyielding, the barrier between you and me.
I see you, but you don't see me, the real me.
That girl is gone.
How does it feel to know that all that once was is now lost?
I see you, but I don't know you, the real you.
I don't even know who "you" are anymore.
It is her, that one girl who I stood up for, and called my friend?
But there's that wall, I can feel it pushing against me.
It's winning, I'm losing.
I tried, I more than tried, but I see her,
And she doesn't even see me anymore.
The wall pushes me back.
I fall down.
I am lost searching for a girl I used to know.
Giving up on some girl I used to know
Forgetting some girl I used to know.

SCREAM

Sometimes being strong is never enough because there are some battles that are invisible to the eye. You don't even know yourself when your tank is empty. You don't know when pushing yourself is too much because there are no bloodstains or bruises. Some battles break your heart. Some battles break your soul. You'll never see when someone is drowning which is why people think they need to give in because it is too much to bear. A silent scream in an empty void. Scream with me, sisters and brothers. You're not alone.

THE GOOD SIR, 2019

I didn't get to say goodbye,
A selfish wish to see your face one more time before you go,
But I missed the last train before you went home.
Home to a place your body and soul will forever rest,
But you were just here in what feels like moments ago.
I see you in my mind, but I can't feel you anymore,
The most loyal and faithful friend.
You always found the good in everything,
And now I know true grief for the first time.
For I reach out my hand and I can feel your spirit holding mine.
You gave us a steadfast ship sailing on a stormy sea,
And the waves never held you back.
I know you can't hold on forever to my hand that doesn't want to let you go,
But I know I can find you in the darkest of nights.
The ones that I wish would have lasted forever,
But I know you're still with me somehow,
Shining down on me from above.
My heart wishes we could go back to the place we met,
But I can just look at the stars and find you shining down on me.
The grief is the darkness separating you from me,
But your light is far too strong and always was.
The good in you extends beyond and I won't forget-
How could I when I know you'll always be there for me?
And when my time finally comes for us to meet again,
I know you'll be waiting for me.
The helping hand to lift me to the sky where only angels like you shine so brightly.
Wait for me there until we meet again.

Grief has no windows and no doors
No way to escape this heavy weight

That makes me feel like I won't ever get up again,
For I'm far too low to the ground
I look at all our pictures and wish I had a million more.
I keep looking at the sky knowing you're looking down on me.
The trouble is you think you have time, but you don't.
And you don't realize that until someone you love is gone.
There isn't an easy way to say goodbye and I don't want to.
So I will let the waves of grief hold onto me as my teacher.
The grief tells me to love more.
The grief tells me to understand more.
The grief tells me to cry more.
Grief is the price we pay for love and when it loses its home, it feels lost.
The only cure for grief is to let the storm pass.
To swim with the ebbs and flows of the ocean grieving with you.
That is until we meet again.

GRIEF HAS NO END POINTS

Grief has no end points.
It's a weight you carry around with you.
You feel it from time to time.
Once the heavy waves pass
You sit by the ocean and wonder
"How am I so dry, yet drowning?"
How does one carry this and live on?
I'm not sure I can stand right now,
But I know I can't stay here.
I need to find my way home.
I don't want to live here anymore.
I want HER and I to move on.
Recovery felt heavy too, but at least there was hope.

Recovery

"The wound is the place the light enters you." - Rumi

GO LOVE HER

Another fire burning goes out.
I really liked this one, but again, I failed.
I look at myself in the mirror.
I see my blue eyes and pale skin.
I see the fire burning in my eyes.
I search for comfort.
I turn on scorching hot water and jump into the shower.
The burning water caresses my skin.
No one to hold me, but the steam and the waterfall of warmth.
I close my eyes and think of what I want.
I want to be successful.
I want to be happy.
And I want to be loved.
The last thought surprises me.
The shower burns me back into reality.
I want to, but I can't stand here forever.
I can't run away, but I can find ways to make me stronger and happier.
As I dry my skin off, I wonder how.
I bare my flaws to the world, outward and inward.
I scrutinize every scar.
"How can anyone love me if I can't even love myself" rolls around in my foggy brain.
I need to wake up.
I need to accept what is and what can be.
I know I've hit another roadblock, but the sun will come out again, once it stops raining.
The fog will clear.
I will see past the scars.
I will accept my flaws.
They are part of who I am.
They do not define me, but they help me realize I am human and to expect perfection is unrealistic.

On the never journey of self-improvement, one may ask "how many times must one fall down and still be expected to get back up?"
The answer is it doesn't matter.
A champion always gets up.
A champion always moves on.
For a true champion knows it's all part of the plan.
Life is so much bigger than the flaws.
Life is so much bigger than all the scars.
I look in the mirror and see myself clearly.
I may never be a ten, but my heart is bigger than all the cons on the list.
It may lead me astray, it may hurt from time to time,
but there's fire in my eyes, my heart, and my soul shines through.
I may not be where I want to be, but I'm closer than I was yesterday.
Life is about progress.
The choice is yours- learn to love yourself for a better tomorrow or never learn to truly love.
For the truth is- you can never really love someone until you find the greatest love of all- yourself.
You are your world.
Love yourself.
Love your flaws.
Love your scars.
Go find yourself.
Go love HER.

BLOOM

It wasn't the light that scared me- though it was blinding me.
It was the darkness-pitch black skies enveloping all my surroundings.
Yes, there was a door; a light shining through the cracks.
The door was meant to be opened.
I felt stuck in the darkness, unable to see anything around me.
I felt so alone here.
Seeing a new door, a new opportunity to escape,
This should have thrilled me.
I should be running towards the light.
Instead I was immobile,
Lost in the emptiness that wasn't just my surroundings,
it was also how I felt inside.
"Who am I?"
I wanted to be in the light, but I had been in the darkness so long.
I forgot what it was like to shine.
I didn't know I had to find the balance between the dark and the light.
I was nothing without both.
I just had to find the in-between,
to feel centered, grounded and whole.
The answers were within, but the journey made me weary.
For this was not the first time I've gone down this road.
Spirit was pushing me and breaking me simultaneously.
I was being renewed, refreshed, reborn again.
But first, we must endure the transformation, the enlightenment, the fulfillment.
This was the journey of life- here we grow again.
A friend once said to me, "Grow through what you go through"
And I was ready to bloom.

A LETTER FOR MY BODY

Dear body,
I'm sorry you feel this way.
I'm sorry you're wired like this.
You've been in survival mode for so long, you don't know any better.
I'm sorry I let you down.
I was just trying to protect you.
It hasn't been easy fighting these demons.
I did this for you.
But now the weary warrior needs to learn how to let go.
How to trust the universe.
How to live to thrive, not survive.
It's normal to make mistakes.
It's normal to be imperfect.
You're human after all
And you didn't deserve this.
I'm sorry you felt like you had to be strong.
I'm sorry you're angry at the world.
I'm sorry you are tired all the time.
I'm sorry when you're heavy from the weight of the world.
I'm sorry you had to go through all of this to find your power.
You are mighty.
You are more powerful than you'll ever know.
You don't have to be on high alert.
Not anymore.
You are protected by the universe.
Your inner child is ready to heal,
She just needs your hand to find the way.

DEAR ONE

"The creative adult is the child who survived" - unknown

Do you see this little girl? Doesn't she look strong? Brave? Powerful? Sassy?

I'm not sure when she lost herself. I'm not sure she remembered her power for a very long time. The darkness was silent; but oh-so-loud. Clouds followed her for so long, everywhere she went.

Those eyes look fearless. I don't remember a time where I wasn't afraid, like her. The confidence in her stature is something I yearn to give back to her.

Regardless of how sad it is that she lost those parts of her, it doesn't mean she could never be found again. That little girl represents innocence, naïveté, and all the good that a child deserves in the world. That little girl is much wiser now. She hasn't been knocked down over and over yet in life in that photo, but she has gotten up over and over again.

The cards we are all dealt are not the same, not even in the same walls. Our experiences shape parts of us, but they never define the whole story.

I love that little girl. She reminds me who I really am. I am not my past, I am my future. I am never lost, I'm always found with her by my side. When I forget what resiliency means, I look at her and remember- I'm doing it all for her. She didn't have the best hand dealt, but she chose to rise above it. She chose to believe that the world had a place for her, despite feeling so little.

Sometimes we carry the weight of the world because we feel like we owe it something. While we should all be grateful that we were given this life, all we owe the world is to try to make it a little bit better than it was before. This doesn't have to be climbing a mountain, but we all do. We all have our mountain to climb. We all will see and feel and experience a multitude of ups and downs. How we react, how we choose our next steps, are the things that define us.

Nobody is going to know the full story. Some parts of it will always be held inside in a safe space. We won't be proud of every step. We won't be proud of every choice, but we can be proud that we made one better than the day before. When you know better, I hope you choose to do better. I could have chosen to continue the cycle. I could have said, "You think you have it bad? You have no idea," and justified what I've seen and learned. But I know in my core that's not okay.

Just because someone hurt you, does not mean others deserve the same treatment- let alone a child. That little girl deserved the world. I carry her with me everyday. I carry how I didn't show up for her, not for lack of trying, but because I was frozen. Frozen in time and space. I lost her because I lost myself. I will never lose you again, my greatest love. "You are the god of your world and you write the script" is one of my favorite lines from "Today is Yours" from The World Within. And when I look at that little girl's face, I believe again. Thank you for trusting me enough to come home again. Home is where I am with you.

IT'S TIME

7-22-15

I thought I was looking for answers, but it turns out I didn't even know what to ask.
My friends, my family- where did they all go?
Nobody is looking out for me.
Nobody is calling my name.
I once stood tall, I was gaining momentum,
but I look in the mirror and see a girl who has lost her way.
I need to feel that fire within me burn.
My broken body is fighting itself and is oh so weary.
I keep thinking I'm going to walk up to the start line a new me, but every time
I get a few steps closer and I fall back ten.
How can I question fate?
How can I stop chance and get what I want out of this life?
I'm only as strong as I think I am.
I am the only one who can truly empower myself.
How much longer must I wait?
How many more times do I have in me?
Will I fall again?
Will I fail again?
I can't live without knowing how far I can make it.
That I gave it my all.

My soul is swirling,
My heart beats relentlessly,
My body is healing.
My feet will find the ground again.
And when I take off,
The world will hear the rumble of thunder with each step.
The lightning in the sky will light the path.
When my heart, mind, body, and soul become one again,
I will find my way home.
Until then, I must be patient.
For the journey ahead will be the most trying, the most demanding.
This time, I will not give in or give up.

It's time to stop dreaming and start being.
Until then, find the stars in the darkness.
Chase the rainbows after the rain.
The past and present are heavy, but the future will be lighter and brighter.
Believe in the journey.
Believe in the burdens and the struggles.
I will achieve because I believe.
It's my time.
Heart, mind, body, and soul- it's time.

SHINE

Some people will never understand.
It's okay if they never will,
As long as you do.
In moments where we seek validation,
Let it come from within.
In moments where we seek peace,
Let it be channeled from within.
And when we cannot find the love we need,
Look in the mirror at your greatest love.
And when we lose our way,
Look in the mirror at your greatest compass.
You can never lose yourself if you build your muscles with not just strength,
But also your own validation, peace, and love.
Your heart, your spirit, your soul are beautiful in your own way.
Some people will never understand this power,
As long as you do, dear one.
As long as you do.
And when you find it, be a light for others so they can find their own path.
In a world where darkness can cloud this power,
You are a star to shine the way.
Shine brightly, dear one.
Shine for HER.

HOME, 2004

I follow the light.
The light in the distance that shines so brightly,
Just like the sun on a clear day.
The everlasting light shines on forever and never ceases to bring me home.
You can never believe what I see because your soul needs to find home.
Follow me, follow me home.
My soul is seeking yours.
Bring me home.
Bring me home.

PEACE

The pain comes in waves, like an ocean.
Some waves swell and splash on the shore, like tears on my pillow.
Deep breaths are hindered by clogged nostrils, full of salt water.

I feel alone on the ocean shore, unsure if I should stay on land or swim into the unknown.
Either way, it's hard to know.
There are seashells that hurt my feet.
There is salt water that will make my wounds burn in the ocean.
If I swim, will I sink or float?
Float long enough and get carried away?
Or sink until I keep drowning and can't breathe anymore?

I look for a sign, anything to make up my mind for me.
Not a single seagull, fish, or friend to help me decide.
I fall down on the hard, wet sand on the shore.
The waves keep splashing and my tears keep the ocean flowing.
So many feelings and emotions trapped inside.
My body, heart, mind, and soul all collide.
Say yes, say no.
Get up, get down.
Nothing makes sense except the pain- constant tears and pain.
"You're no quitter," your mind says.
"Don't let go," your heart says.
A heavy body and a heavy soul waits for a command.
My arms clutch my knees to my chest,
Alone I cry, torn between two worlds.
I look behind and see emptiness,
but also a firm surface I can walk away on.
Before me, the water comes in cycles- first calm, then crashing before me.
"Get up," your mind says.
I crawl forward on my knees and look to the sky.
There are dark clouds above me enveloping both land and sea.
Unsure still, I struggle to my feet, and take steps between both worlds.
I close my eyes, and remember why I hurt and cry,
"I choose me" your heart says.
I pause and look at the waves, curious as to what could be, but unless those waves come following after me,
It's safe to stay on my own two feet.
My feet start to sink in the sand, and with each step, so does my heart and body.
But my mind and soul know I can find balance and calm again.
When I no longer need to look behind me anymore.
And this gives me peace.
Oh, this gives me peace.

Shay, 2014

BABY STEPS, 2014

Am I a feminist?
Or does society just think so because I'm not okay with the status quo?
I'm a size 2, but I don't believe it.
I see nothing but scars and cellulite.
Somehow, I still smile.
Somehow, I still rise above and find ways to love me.
Society, you drove me to hatred of the one person I need to love the most, myself.
My heart and my soul are so weary, but I am proud.
Size 14 to size 2.
I battled sadness.
I gave up things I wanted.
I sacrificed.
I learned what it meant to be strong-
To find strength,
To find a voice inside of me.
Who I wanted to be, and still yet to become.
To rejoice in the small victories.
The baby steps were just the beginning.
The foundation of the building blocks of life.
Baby steps may last years before you can see any hint of the finish line.
It's easy to neglect those you love on the pathway to success.
Never forget those who love you unconditionally.
Never forget those who supported you on your way.
We are inherently selfish.
We long and lust for things and people that may not even matter the next day you wake up.
We use and abuse.
We take and never return the favor.
Remember to say, "I love you."
Remember to say, "Thank you."

Remember to never give up.
We are all human.
We will fail.
It is those that can endure the pain and disappointment.
Those who can endure the negligence and voices in your head that hold you back.
You will rise to the occasion.
You will hold your head high.
You may fall down again,
But you will let it go.
You will refuse to let the world get better of you.
You don't listen to the critics.
They don't know how far you've come.
They don't know how much farther you've made it from the starting line.
Just remember compromise-
You are not Superman or Wonder Woman.
You are not invincible or immortal in this human body on this earth.
We are beautifully flawed- magnificent creatures of imperfection.
What made you stop believing in magic?
Just because the world does not always stand in your corner,
Just because you feel alone when push comes to shove,
Just because people want to break you, hurt you, tear you apart,
This does not mean we live in a world without magic.
We are all lost souls with broken wings.
We cannot fly until we know how to get home.
We cannot go home until we heal ourselves.
The winds howl words of discouragement.
Can you let it go?
Is it too much for you?
Let it go.
Let go of the negative voices in your head.
Your own worst enemy is you.
Find the voice in your head.
The voice is your heart.

The purpose of your heart is to feel and to be felt.
One of the greatest battles is finding agreement between your head and your heart.
You will choose in favor of logic some days, others lust or longing.
You will learn from your mistakes.
Let go of your past for it is too heavy for your soul.
Your mind, your heart- your whole body- will suffer.
Learn, live, and let go.
It is better to have loved,
Loved in everything you are than have never loved at all.
The world and bad days seem better when you have someone at your side, but is it them, or the idea of them, that brings you comfort?
We are all human- we will misunderstand, have anxiety, and be taken advantage of.
When two worlds collide, two hearts that love differently,
Two minds that think differently- it is a beautiful chaos that invigorates everything we are.
You can't control a lot of things in this life- where you come from or where your ultimate starting line begins,
but what you can control, your decisions, your attitude, your reputation- this is what makes you- you.
If you are closer today than you were yesterday,
If you're trying, if you are resilient,
If you love, learn, let go, and remember the journey,
You can look back and be proud.
You can say, "I lived."
Does it matter what the world thinks of me, or just those who matter the most to me think?

HER

Too often, we let the past define us.
Now, those people who judged me probably wouldn't even recognize me.
I have transformed.
I have evolved.
I said goodbye to the old me, and now I'm so much farther than I thought I'd ever be.
It will never be enough.
I'll keep pushing for this notion of perfection,
For it is what keeps me going.
Trying to be better than I was the day before.
Time flies and life will throw you curveballs.
Are you going to step up to the plate?
You might strike out.
You might get some scars along the way,
But they don't define you.
Let that fire and passion shine in your eyes.
Become who you want to be by leaning into the best version of yourself.
Most days, the lows will outweigh the highs.
Rejoice in those moments where you feel alive.
You feel happy.
You feel joy.
Even the days you feel down, rejoice in the fact that you feel anything at all.
You no longer disassociate.
You are no longer numb.
You are a goddamn queen.
Look how far you've come.

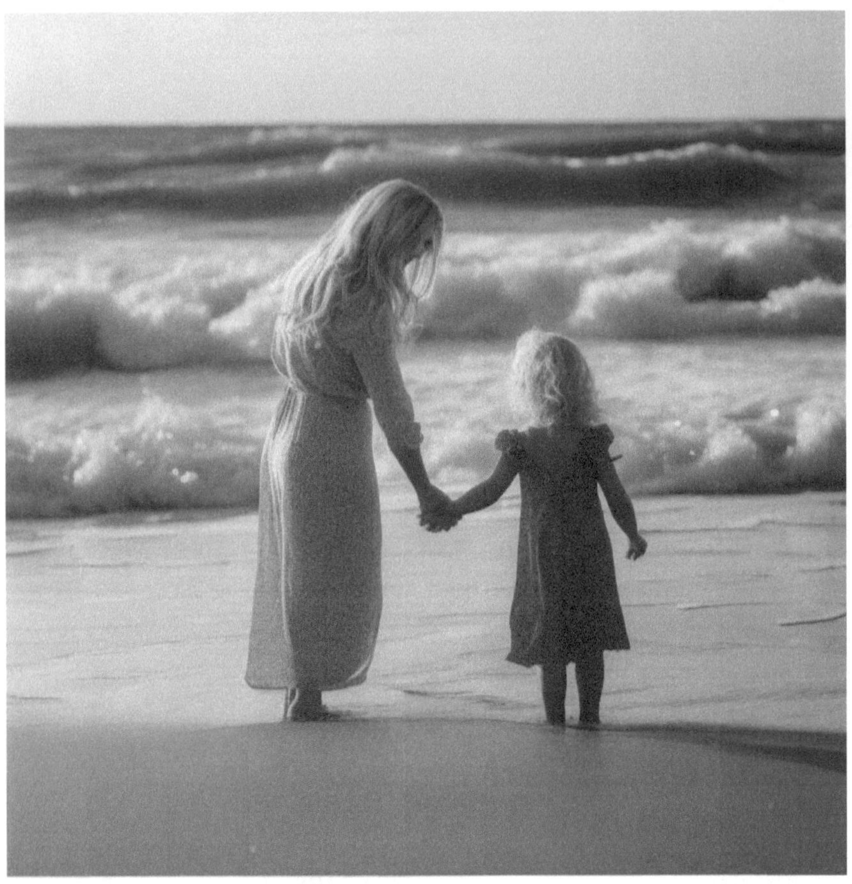

Finding HER was always going to be the greatest adventure.
Finding HER was always going to be the best thing you've ever done.
Finding HER for HER was everything.

FINISH LINE, 6/23/15

On the never ending journey of self-improvement, you begin to wonder how many times you can fall down and still be expected to get back up.

I have visions of dreams,

I see them, I taste them, and I struggle.

I've accepted where I am in life.

And some days, the weight of reality is too heavy for our little bones and muscles to carry. On those days, it is okay to close your eyes and find peace by believing tomorrow will be a little lighter of a load to carry. Even if it is not true and the struggle will continue, at least you have hope.

Some days you get so caught up in life, you forget how blessed you are. Your world revolves around you, but it would not continue to spin without your family and friends.

You know who you are. You defy gravity. You pick me up when I am down. Your love and support is endless. You are an army I'm proud to march beside. I am never alone because I always carry you with me.

You know me. You know how much pride I have. How stubborn I am. This is a road I must go alone, but I know you'll be there for me when I lose my way and need a friend. For that, I am ever grateful. I hope you'll be there waiting for me at the finish line.

NEXT CHAPTER

You have a bucket of water to easily put my fire out, but you would rather watch me burn. You didn't make me. The fire did. So when you say that I've never suffered compared to the likes of you, I will show you my battle scars only once. I have nothing left to prove to you. The bridges behind me will burn, just like any memories I have left of you. Sometimes the earth must be scorched to be reborn anew. You're not welcome in my next chapter, even if it means I walk alone.

COME AWAY WITH ME

Come away with me to a land that only exists in my mind,
To a place where quietude is the only thing that rules,
To a place where the shoreline is everlasting,
To a place where respect is for every single person,
To a place where it doesn't matter who you are,
To a place where you can rest in peace.
Come away with me to a land of joy,
To a land of fantasy,
To an exotic island,
To a place where you can live without worry,
To a place where your heart can love unapologetically,
Come away with me in my dreams.

Shay, 2005

TONIGHT, December 10th, 2021

In moments of darkness, I no longer fear the shadows.
For I am divinely guided.
In moments of painful sadness, I no longer fear the weight,
For there is nothing I can no longer carry.
In moments of despair, I no longer falter.
Staying stuck prevents me from moving forward.
In moments of my C-PTSD flashbacks and memories,
I remember I am safe and grounded-
For the universe protects me from everything that is not for my highest good.
This wall I see blocking my path ahead,
This door of blinding light,
Tonight is the night.
Tonight I walk into my future.

THINGS I WISH I WAS TOLD:

1. Your sister will be your best friend. If you don't have a sister, it's okay. You will find several non-biological sisters as you get older. It is important to cherish these relationships and nurture them.

2. If someone makes you feel less than you are, they are uncomfortable with themselves. In this case, you are not the problem. They are.

3. It's okay if you never fit in a size 2 pair of jeans. Barbies and models present a pretty picture, but the majority of females in America are not built to be a size 2. Eating healthy is an important habit as is exercising regularly, but your body is your own. We are all made differently. Don't compare yourself to anyone else.

4. Speaking up in a group is hard. Especially for young girls and women who are afraid of being wrong and saying the wrong thing. It's okay to be wrong. We are learning and growing together. If someone makes fun of you for trying, ask them why they haven't spoken up or tried yet.

5. It's easy to get down on yourself. Society is hard on females for their behavior, their looks, and it builds expectations in our mind of how we are supposed to present ourselves. Find someone who you can trust to talk to about these feelings. This may be a friend or a family member, or even a teacher. Don't hold it all inside and don't be afraid to share your emotions.

6. When you're young, it's hard to understand how your body will change over time. One day, you will need to start wearing a bra and deodorants. You'll want to start shaving your legs and try on makeup. Over time, if you don't like any of these new things, don't feel obligated to wear lipstick or eye shadow everyday. Just be comfortable in your own skin or as much as possible. Breathe and

remember, it's a phase of life where you are discovering who you are and who you want to be. You'll find that with time.

7. Don't be afraid to ask questions. If someone shuts you down, find someone else you can go to. Not everyone is a good parent or teacher or mentor. We all have our strengths and weaknesses. Learn to accept who wants to help you. There are plenty of people out there who do. You just have to find the right ones.

8. Everything is temporary. Feelings and people and time. It all goes away. There is a lot of pressure to succeed. The sooner you find your passions and strengths, the sooner you will be on your path to success. Keep your head up. The road will not always be straight or smooth, but the journey is what counts when you're preparing for what the future brings.

9. Not everyone will be cheering for you. Unfortunately, as time goes on, you'll see some of your cruelest critics be your female peers and perhaps former friends who you once called you an ally. People who are not confident and uncomfortable with their success and their bodies do not want you to feel comfortable. They want you to feel the same as they do to make them feel better about themselves. Find your tribe, ignore the cruelty, and stay focused on your goals.

10. My biggest regret is not believing in myself. The time I lost and wasted justifying decisions that held me back in my goals and dreams are wasted on a lack of belief in myself. If you want to do something and you can't think about anything else, then you're probably meant to. Even if you don't succeed, better to try and fly than stay on the ground, wondering about all the places I could have gone. If you take nothing else away from this, remember it is never too late to accomplish your dreams.

11. Dignity and intelligence are just as sexy as beauty. If a man tells you otherwise, he is not a man. He is a boy who needs to grow up.

Some boys never grow up. Avoid these like the plague. They are not worthy of you.

12. If I were a boy instead of girl with the knowledge that I know now, I would be kind to any female suffering from PMS. The first year is especially rough and usually during middle school. It's no joke and I would be kind knowing that it is painful and messy. It's easier to empathize when you have felt the same struggle. It is difficult to relate to any person's pain and suffering, but we can still be kind and not assume negativity.

13. Your voice matters. There will be days you feel brave. There will be days you feel worthless. This is the cycle of life and growing up. Say something when you don't feel comfortable. Speak up if you think something is wrong. Be brave. It is harder than anything else in today's world for a little girl or a young woman to find her voice, but you never will if you don't start speaking up for yourself. Take a big breath. You can do it.

2018

FREE, 9-17-21

And when the mountains grew, the sea rose, and the planet began,
There wasn't sadness or fear of a new beginning.
It felt refreshing- the crisp air filled with clarity and a fresh start.
The chance to begin again with no baggage and no weight.
A child shouldn't have to stand at the starting line carrying the weight of the world.
A child should get a chance where there is no grief or shame.
So now, as a reborn version of yourself, it's time to empty the backpack.
We stand at a new starting line.
We stand in our power together, hand in hand.
My inner child is so proud of how far we've come.
We hug-excited to have finally reunited as one.

We are worthy.
We are strong.
We are ready for love.
We love ourselves.
We no longer need validation from others to feel worthy.
We embrace our inner voice, love, and spirituality.
Everything we ever wanted is coming.
Everything we've ever dreamed of is on its way.
Hand in hand, we take our first step together-
Releasing any fear, guilt, or shame.
We will never let anyone hurt us again- only light and love allowed.
We are kind, understanding, and responsive.
We know what it's like to carry too much.
We are free.
We are healed.
We are one.

PROUD, JUNE 12TH, 2022

Standing in your power should never bring you shame.
Speaking your truth should never bring you guilt.
Do you remember, dear one, when you walked alone?
Barefoot, on a path with no directions, carrying the weight of the world?
Do you remember the darkness that engulfed your light when you were afraid to shine?
You are more than the shame and the guilt of the trauma you carry, but never should have endured.
You are a child of the universe that loved,
Beyond this land, this planet, these people.
One day this journey will all make sense.
YOU should be SO PROUD.

SILENCE

4-22-23

I've spent most of my life keeping my mouth shut.
I was taught to live in fear,
To not draw attention to myself, to be a fly on the wall.
With that comes great listening and observation skills,
But a blocked throat chakra.
Someone who clams up and is afraid.
Someone who struggled to keep her voice steady when standing up and speaking out.
Perhaps the silence has made the delivery more angry than it should be.
I'm aware of that rage inside,
But what's that saying when the quiet ones do have something to say?
My childhood friend's mom used to say to me - "It's always the quiet ones."
In retrospect, I think what she was saying was that there was more to me than met the eyes.
When I look back, there were always people who believed in me,
It was just never the ones you were supposed to have on lock.
This was the beginning of the damaged inner child,
Who never really had the chance to thrive-
So now, I must stand up, speak up, and carry on for her.
It's our time and I've got something to say.
The real question was never if I was ready,
It was always whether or not the rest of the world was.
Some people find their voice as a child,
Others much later in their journey.
When you can find that voice within, stand in your power, and speak your truth.
It doesn't matter what they all say.
For this is all winning the most important fan in the audience over-
That little girl who has been patiently waiting with fire in her eyes.

The tears glaze over, the clouds lift, and we are one again.
Pain and sadness are no longer needed here.
The journey ahead is one where this body, mind, and soul are free from the chains of the past.
And if we should ever get lost again, little one-
I will crawl to the ends of the earth to find you.
I will never lose you again.
It was meant to be a struggle, a journey, a pathway to find this new version of self,
A new page, a new chapter-
A brand new book.
One where the fire burns bright and the ashes of the past blow away in the distance.
There's no going back now.
The universe lit a new fire in my soul, reminding me that everything happens in divine timing,
And no matter what or when or how- I can still have it all.
For this was all meant for me- to learn, to grow, and now I am FREE.
I am ME.

DEAR UNIVERSE

Dear Universe,
I accept all the lessons you've been sending me.
I understand that I am worthy.
I love myself.
I am fulfilled and find self-actualization within.
I no longer look outside myself for love, fulfillment, or validation.
I am the best version of myself.
Chakras flowing- stronger than ever-
My house is safe and secure.
I am grateful for everything you've shown me.
I'm ready to move on.
I am leveling up thanks to your divine guidance, showing me how to lead with love and light.
I love myself.
I am proud of myself.
I am ready for my soulmate, my twin flame.
I welcome them into my life as my true partner-
We give each other time and space to find ourselves.
Together, we serve the divine and are fulfilled by your love.
I am love.
I am worthy of being loved by another.
I am ready and willing.
I am grateful.
Thank you, thank you, thank you.
So be it, so it is.

STALKER

I'm not a book that you can translate, or put into your own words.
I wrote the book, I wrote the script,
Don't you dare try to plagiarize.
You were promising like a new pair of shoes,
Shiny on the outside, but you never quite fit.
You'll never fit right, why do you even try?
You use her to break my heart, but I am above any childish game you play.
She loves me more than you.
She doesn't even know you.
I don't even know you.
But I know HER.
And she loves me more.
She'll always love me more.
Your heart is broken and lying in the midst with all of your lies.
But you threw it all away without knowing the consequences.
Don't give what you're not prepared to take back.
Don't fall in love with those who have more to them than you could ever know.
You'll never know me now.
I'll never let you know me.
So leave me alone from the distance you watch me from
While I become everything you could have ever hoped for.

JOB DESCRIPTION

For the last time, I heard a litany of all the grief and pain that I've caused you. You are so removed from reality, you can't see how hard it is for me to just keep breathing. You made the choice to put me here. I did nothing but find ways to flight or fight, but mostly flight, because I didn't know how to break myself free from your prison. The poison of your words does nothing but make me ill. My heart forgets how to keep going sometimes because of all the times I held my breath around you. My body falls into dizzy spells often because I spent more years falling down then standing up. It is not used to fighting, but you've left me no choice. I am no longer your punching bag anymore that you obsessively attacked and tried to control because it is the only way to ease your self-loathing.

Can't you see what you've done? You care more about winning a battle than the health and wellness of a child? Isn't that part of the job description? To love and care for and support? I learned none of these things from you, but seeing the opposite put me on a path to love, to care for, and to support others. These are my people. These are my family. Your obsession and self-hate and jealousy are not welcome here. And yet you keep acting like you own me. I was never yours to own or abuse or treat like an object. I was a child, forced to grow up in an unstable environment, and I barely escaped. What makes you think I would ever go back to a place where my memory serves no more in photos, just a swirling dark cycle of endless denial and hate because I was the one who found the light? It was not because you couldn't. It was because you never wanted to. The light you steal from others may keep you going on, but I will never return to the darkness of my past that nearly killed me. You like being the victim, I like being the hero. I will not surrender to you. My survival guide is so that others like me can make it too. I'm the hero of my own story, and you are not welcome here anymore. This is the letter I'm wasting on you.

DAY ONE

"There can be no rebirth without a dark night of the soul, a total annihilation of all that you believed in and thought that you were."- Pir Vilayat Inayat Khan

Four years ago, I felt annihilated. My life changed dramatically when my normal was taken away from me. My new normal was a re-injured surgically repaired meniscus, several bulging discs in my neck and back and a hernia in my neck that wouldn't let me sleep without my hands and arms going numb. It was like a fog, with dark clouds over me as I waded from doctor's office to doctor's office. I don't know how I made it to work when all I wanted was the pain to go away and to stay in bed. I couldn't start physical therapy until about six months post-injuries because of the pain and when I did-it was brutal. The kind of pain that makes you question if it was worth it- or if anything was.

After a year of PT, 1-3X a week with the chiropractor, and more shots then I can count, the pain wasn't going away and I had to have neck and back surgery. I tried really hard to avoid it, but I had so much nerve damage it was the only way to stop my migraines and pain- even for just a little while. There were days the most exercise I could do was take a short walk down by the water and think about all the Day Ones in my life and that One Day may not be an option anymore. I was told that I may not be able to play volleyball again and boxing was done. So I had to make a choice- keep trying and start over with another Day One, or keep wondering about finding normal again One Day. I understood that 2015 normal was not coming back and the old Shay was not either. All I knew was I needed something to believe in again, and the only way to do this was to say goodbye to the old version of myself. So I kept going to PT and the chiro after my surgery. I kept trying to crawl, to walk, and to believe that One Day I could run again. I can't tell you the number of Day Ones I went through. I had to start over several times. It was truly emotionally, mentally and physically exhausting, but there was a voice in my head that's always been there. It told me that quitting was not in my DNA and today and everyday moving forward was not going to be Day One of being something I was not. I had to convince myself that there was a finish line and no matter how many Day Ones it took, I could be reborn into the next best version of myself.

When I look back, I'm grateful. For without the unforgiving pain, the scars and the challenges, I would not be as strong or as proud as I am today. The old version of Shay will walk with me forever. She reminds me of the strength I found to evolve, transform, and believe that "I may win, I may lose, but I'll never be defeated." There are those who have suffered much more than me. It is important when someone is brave enough to share their trauma, you know this is not a competition. Four years was a long time. They say "someone who drowns in seven feet of water is just as dead as someone who drowns in 20 feet." I hope by sharing this with you there is a takeaway that our worst days may still come, but there is a new version of you waiting after every hill and mountain we have to climb. I hope that if there is someone out there who needs someone to believe in them- I see you and although I may not understand your pain- hope is the only thing stronger than fear. I hope you know you're not alone and you can do this. Maybe you feel like you are drowning, grieving a loved one, running the marathon of life, or the greatest challenge of all- finding yourself- but, it is never too late to start over. And when you do, the old version of you will be waiting at the finish line to remind you of how far you have come. We will continue to evolve as long as we keep taking steps forward. The doctors told me no, and so did the old Shay. Today I won, regardless of what place, because I beat the version of me that was holding me back. So what's it going to be for you- One Day or Day One?

THE RIDE

I'm not sure what I was expecting, but it certainly wasn't this. What might have been or could have been doesn't really matter because the days go by with the blink of an eye. Yesterday's memories fly by in the rear view mirror and time is unforgiving. We keep being pushed forward, whether we are ready or not. I want to control the path, but there's not much of the rope I can grab, I can conquer. It keeps dragging me along, and I'm hanging on for dear life. There are so many people just watching from a distance, but not many willing to help you on your feet as you keep holding on. Some people aren't brave enough, some people don't like you enough, and some people think you aren't worthy enough. These "some" people aren't your friends, family, or tribe. They are there because they want you to quit, to fail, to fall behind, because they're barely hanging on just like you. They may look like they're doing it better than you from a distance, but deep down we are all struggling and fighting to hang on. So if we are all in this together, why don't we help each other hang on? Time doesn't care about the color of your skin, the god you worship, your gender, or age. Time is the only true enemy we all have as we try to figure out our why. Surely it was not to hate one another for the differences between us. Why not help each other? Hang on a little tighter, instead of hoping someone else falls before you do? If time is the enemy, why do you want your fellow human beings to fail? The only competition we have is with time, and that we find ourselves before our time runs out.

We all hurt. We all bleed. We're all human. But there are those moments where you forget your limitations. Moments where you lift off, soar and feel so alive. But then, there are those moments where you never leave the ground. There are moments where the wind isn't strong enough, you crash, and you don't make it. You were so confident. You believed the world was in the palm of your hand. "Not now," says Life. "It's not your time," says Life.

Life says you need to be more humble. You need to learn from failure. You need to understand you deserve absolutely nothing. You have to try and try again. This is where a master succeeds. From failing so many times, it becomes second nature. This is where the second wind kicks in. A second chance to lift off. Do you feel the breeze? Are you strong enough to make it? The first step is the hardest, getting back on the road of life. There's no one cheering for you on the side of the road. You have to make the decision to take that first step. Are you brave enough to take it? I promise, take one more step, and you will never look back.

Set yourself free from the pain, the failures, and the misery. You can make it if you believe. Here's to you, the one who didn't give up, even when no one else believed. Hope is the only thing stronger than fear. There's no promise I won't crash again. That I will not fail again. But if you never try, you'll never know, and I already lived with too many regrets. Tell me no? I'll just push harder. You can't break me. If someone is going to break me, it's going to be me. This is my life, my rules, my destiny. Watch me fly, watch me fail. I don't care. Judge me, laugh at me. But I'd rather die knowing I tried my damndest than live knowing I was too afraid to take one more step. See you on the road, kid. Let me know if you're down for a ride. It's time to resurge.

MAY 2020

A year ago today, my stalker showed up to a public event to confront me. I had been avoiding this person for months and not speaking to them, hoping they would catch the hint and leave me the hell alone. They had been desperately sending things to my workplace because I purposely moved so they didn't have my address because I was so afraid of them. Because I was so involved in the community, they knew I would be there.

An hour passes as I wander around, seeing my friends. Then, I see them. I am shocked and filled with dread. Thank goodness I could hide in the VIP tent as I processed what to do. I called my sister because that morning I had a sixth sense thinking to myself what if they showed up. Sure enough, my inkling turned out to be my biggest nightmare.

I ran to my car under the cover of tents. I called my sister in tears, devastated that I couldn't enjoy my event because this person wouldn't leave me alone. I am not a crier, so when I say I was crying hysterically, I was crying hysterically.

Unsure of what to do, I drove to the parking lot across the street from the police office. With the help of my siblings, I drove across the street and entered the police office. I want to reiterate the fear and helplessness I was feeling at this moment. The same office I did my ride along with during the Citizen's Academy, so I was filled with hope someone could help me. Anyone.

I didn't want to enter because I was afraid they wouldn't believe me- and boy, was I right. He thought I was an annoying teenager and was shocked when I stated I was the chairperson of the board. And sure enough, I was told that I couldn't be helped because there wasn't an imminent threat. Public events are welcome to the public and none of what I said was enough to even have them put a report on file to put me at ease for the next time. Bottom line, he said to go downtown if I wanted to file an injunction, but that was the extent of help I was getting. As I continue to cry and try to process that my ally couldn't help me, I wobble back to my car. The fear I had, driving to my home, wondering if they had my new address. My head is pounding as this was a scary road to go down again alone.

I left and contacted a lawyer friend. My brother came over for moral support and said he would go with me if I wanted to headquarters and to get an injunction. But the shock of the event and imminent trauma overcoming my body came in the form of a migraine and I couldn't leave my sofa. I could feel the fear, the shock, and the emotions enveloping my body.

I soon learned that injunctions would require my address to be included in the information, so if I did file one, my stalker would know where I lived. There are some exceptions to the rule, but the thought of having to share my story again was far too much to bear. Knowing I had to try to go tell my story again to a different station because the police officer wouldn't take my report was also the most defeated feeling I've ever had in my life. I was frankly devastated that an office I so highly regarded flat out rejected me.

So you're probably wondering why I'm sharing this with you, and it is certainly not for your pity. I'm sharing this because law enforcement is an extremely critical partner to building safe communities. That being said, there are so many very gray areas we, and especially women, need to be aware of.

The truth is there will always be bad people and a lot of criminals know these gray areas and will cross the line up until the point before it reaches legitimate criminal activity. They are smart enough to press your buttons just enough before they could ever get caught. This is the same as white supremacists putting hate speech all over the public sidewalks outside a synagogue, knowing they could never be caught.

Verbal, emotional, and psychological trauma and abuse are so very real. This same person is the reason I have fibromyalgia. It's frankly a devastating disability that encompasses more than 100 different symptoms. My fibromyalgia was triggered by this person's verbal and emotional abuse months before this even happened.

I am not ashamed to share this story. My only regret is that I allowed this person to continue to be in my life so long it created the fibromyalgia monster within me. I should have been braver. I should have spoken out sooner. I should have walked away sooner. But when your mind is poisoned by social norms, you want to believe that certain people have your best interests in mind. They don't. There is no free card to your inner circle. Whether it be a husband, a friend, a parent, a boss, you do not need to endure torture because a person in authority abuses their power.

I may have suffered and endured a lot in this life, but I've never felt stronger or more empowered or prouder than I do now. Keeping your head above water is so much harder when you're carrying around baggage you never should have had in the first place. It's not your job to fix other people. Some things in life cannot be fixed. Some things in life can only be carried. Scars, blood, sweat, and tears, I'm a fibromyalgia warrior, a strong woman, and a brave soldier. This is why I am the way I am.

BREATHE

Up and down.
This is the journey of life.
One moment you're blessed to be alive.
The next you're on your knees in despair.
All one can do is find in-between balance.
This is the reality of being human.
Life is not beautiful because every day is magical.
Beauty is feeling all of humanity inside one body, mind, and soul.
There is growth in all of the light and dark moments.
Peace isn't a permanent destination, it's a feeling when you made it through another day.
All you have to do is remember to breathe.

DO IT

March 12th, 2007

As a young woman in the world full of vanity, lies, and destruction,
I've learned and realized that life is full of possibilities and reasons.
Reasons why people fail, die, get up again, and are born.
Born to fulfill their destinies or to fall down and lose all track of time and faith and reason.
A long time ago I would have thought nothing of how or who runs a country,
But once you reach a certain age,
You see things differently
Life is full of choices.
Life is different now, with more responsibilities.
Maybe life has planned how you were meant to impact the world,
Or maybe, just maybe, you can have the chance of reaching just a tiny bit higher,
And reach just a tiny bit farther,
And even if you impact one life,
That one life could be the change that we need in the world.

CARRY ON

There's a place down the hall and around the corner. It asks me for my name and I'll follow you down. It says it knows what I'm looking for, but I can't see the end, I came for the journey. I don't know where I'm going, but that's okay. I never really knew before either, just trying to find the right path to guide me home. I never knew a place like that before- where I could rest and close my eyes without fear. I've come from a land that knows no mercy, which is why I know where I'm going will never be as bad as where I've been. There are signs on this path, but no one to ask directions. Just the words of people mumbling along as I go.

Perhaps I'm really going nowhere. Perhaps I'm never finding a place. All I know is that forward is always better than backwards, so I will carry on.

SELF

All my life I had been looking for something, and everywhere I turned
Someone tried to tell me what it was.
I accepted their answers, too,
though they were often self-contradictory.
I was naïve.
I was looking for myself and asking everyone except myself questions
which I, and only I, could answer.
It took me a long time to achieve a realization everyone else appears
to have been born with: that I am nobody but myself.
So why do I keep asking other people who have no idea who I really am?

THE IN-BETWEEN

Oh trauma, your dark black ugly hands keep me pulled down,
Down where my grief still ebbs and flows like the waves of the ocean,
The endless water goes on and on, and so do all the emotions I try to hold inside.
Some days strong, some days sad,
Some days I wish I didn't even know how to breathe,
But that was before I let go.
I can't recover with your invisible hands wrapped around my neck.
You can't even see how tight your grip is, and I can barely breathe.
The only way out is to escape, because this is just a game to you.
There are no winners here, just you sitting on a throne made of thorns that do nothing but hurt me every time I have to kneel before you.
What I thought was my home was really my prison that did nothing but hold me back.
The chains I broke weren't easy to break, and neither was accepting the fact that all I knew of love was a lie.
Love maybe was not patient, nor was it always kind, and I'll never forgive you for making me believe that no one could love me.
All you ever did was make the battle of finding self-love unsteady and formidable, but isn't that what you wanted?
But when I finally broke free and found the summit, and I saw the blue of the sky and the brightness of the sun and stars, I knew there was no going back.
That side of the mountain nearly killed me, but I was not going to put my fate back in the hands of someone who made me believe I was not worthy of love.
I wait at the summit for the storm to come; the rain falls and cleanses my skin.
It may not be able to wash away all the trauma, but it does heal the part of me that needs to believe I am worthy enough to leave this all behind.

The tears and the rain are steady, but they will pass, as bad times always do.
I close my eyes until it stops; then, I will be ready.
Standing before a path of the unknown, I open my eyes.
There's no fear here. I can't worry about something I can't control, but I can control my next step.
My next step would be forward as I was never going back again; nothing could be worse than where I've been.
With a deep breath and a broken heart, I watch the sky clear.
The blue emerges amid the clouds and I am born again.
The colors light my path and the sun shines down, calling me to find my new home.
And if there was any sliver of doubt left, a rainbow breaks through the clouds to welcome me.
The first step is always the hardest, but the lights and spirits were guiding me.
I didn't know where I was going, but it didn't matter,
For the sun and the stars did, and that was all I needed to know that this was where I belonged.
With every step, I feel lighter and lighter. There was no one and nothing left that could ever hold me back again.
I was a warrior and I needed to keep going, because I knew there were others who were once lost like me.
I would keep this path lit until I could no longer breathe.
This was the only way the trauma, the grief, and the recovery would be worth it.
I was a spark that caught on fire; the embers and glow burned relentlessly in me.
That was the only peace I would ever know; that my steps and words lit fires for others who suffered like me.
I had to help them find the light that saved me, even if it was just one little girl who needed a glimmer of hope.
Maybe I would even be lucky enough to meet her one day.
As I'm now running down my path, I find a waterfall.
As I walk closer, I see a little girl; she's smiling at me.

Finally, I got close enough to see her face and she was me; the face was mine.
She was that little girl who felt like nothing.
She was that little girl who needed someone to save her.
I'm so sorry it took me so long, but I did find her again.
I reach my hand out to her; we laugh and we cry.

I know she forgives me for we both finally had a home that was safe and free.
I don't want to let her go, but I know I have to, or else neither of us can move on.
For we are one somehow and we are never losing each other again.
Home is not a place, it is a feeling.

For you were my last broken piece to put me back together.
My mind and my heart are home again, with you by my side.
We can finally celebrate, for all is finally well with my soul.
Come now little girl, it is time to resurge.

DONE

This is the year I parent myself
It's time to change what I think
I'm not going to lose my job
Everything is going to be fine
Everything is going to work out the way it should
I'm always taken care of
I'm provided for
The universe will never take someone away from me unless it's better that way
You've had too many people dragging you down, don't let yourself be one of them.
You're the only person you've ever needed.
Quiet your mind, breathe, and trust.
Everything is falling into place behind the scenes.
When they said, "Every action has an equal, yet opposite reaction"
It wasn't science,
It was life.

BRAVE

Where is the finish line?
The one you finally cross when you're proud of yourself?
The one where you can finally feel worthy?
Each time you get close, it seems to move further in the distance.
So maybe it's not a thing, an accomplishment, a moment.
Maybe it's the journey, and each time you make a new level, that's enough.
Maybe being worthy isn't a destination.
So stop running.
Stop climbing a mountain.
Stop killing yourself.
Instead, take a breath, a pause, a moment.
Think about where you stood a year ago.
Wasn't there something in those 365 days that made you smile?
Wasn't there something that made you proud?
Wasn't there a moment you felt more alive?
Celebrate the small steps, every breakthrough, each level.
Compare yourself to no one.
Just keep moving forward, but this time instead, don't forget that you chose to be something more than your yesterday.
This is brave, courageous, and worthy.
This is your moment.

TRUTH

How quickly the excitement of today becomes the yearnings of yesterday.
Building expectations of nothingness because reality was just a tease.
You had hope that things were finally going to change.
But wait, it's just another failed chance at what could have been.
They say when things don't work out it is because they weren't meant to.
But nobody told you how many times you get to live with the disappointment of yesterday.
For it felt so real.
Like this time you were going to win.
Is it karma?
Did I deserve this because in another life I was cruel?
I have yet to find the answer.
They say to look within to find happiness and joy and love.
So why does everyone look everywhere else first?
Expectations versus reality is the silent killer of this life.
You can't expect a life free of disappointment when you're an imperfect human surrounded by much worse.
The only truth at the end of the day is that the only person you can rely on is yourself.
"People aren't good, they're just trying to be," you said.
Ain't that the goddamn truth.

THE PHOENIX

Sometimes the air you breathe isn't oxygen.
Not when you're drowning.
Sometimes it's a voice saying they believe you.
Sometimes it's someone sitting next to you in the dark.
In the blackness, you find monsters that could never see the light of day.
For they are far too dark.
But, they live within the walls of your flesh and bone.
But, they crawl inside when you just can't keep going on.
Sometimes even the divine must be reminded of how human they are.
For without it, what are we?
Sometimes the lessons are greater than the pain.
Sometimes the next right thing is greater than what you thought you couldn't live without.
The light always wins.
No matter how many times the sun sets.
No matter how many times you fall down again into the hole you try to keep escaping.
For when you do,
Sit with the darkness a little bit longer.
Sit with the imperfections and the failings.
Even works of art are made by imperfect humans.
So when you think about giving in,
So when you think about letting go,
Remember how many more times you've escaped the darkness and found the light.
Remember how many more times you've survived what you thought you couldn't.
Rising from ashes over and over.

This is the purpose of the Phoenix.
This is the life of the warrior.
Stop holding your breath.
Amazing awaits.

THE HEALER

She came to me at my lowest.
A goddess who knew exactly what I needed.

She gave me the gifts of grace, kindness, and understanding.
She came to me with love, gratitude, and light.
She came to me because it was time, time to begin again.
She will rise again like a Phoenix.
All stars burn before they shine.
Everything makes sense in the end.
Here's to Round 2.
Here's to Worthy 2.0.

INVISIBLE ILLNESS

A little slow, a little broken, and a lot differently abled.
Every day is a new adventure, a new symptom, a new problem.
But it doesn't matter because when the sun goes up, it's okay if my best is my best.
The expectations aren't moving targets, setting me up to fail, or breaking me down.
The pain is bearable because I have the spirit of belief ingrained in me.
They tell me good job, that they're impressed, that I'm invaluable.
It's a lot easier to bear it all when your team lifts you up for you as a person.
No matter the scars, the struggles, and the pain.
You find peace reminded by the wholeness of the unique person you are.
A little kindness, a little humanity, and a lot of belonging.
Makes someone feel a little better, a little stronger, a little bigger.
Be a light in the darkness- for the world of a disabled person needs all the light and warmth we can find.
We are not welcome in most places without speculation, unwelcome questions, and judgment.
We just want to belong, to be good enough, and to find a place in a world.
Help us, don't hinder us.
Embrace us, don't push us away because it takes a little more effort.
You can change our lives if you push yourself a little more.
Please believe us when we tell you that we can't do something.
That our energy or body can't handle it.
Sometimes it's our mind that worries if we will make it.
That battle between mind, body, and soul can be a lot to handle.
Our humanness is a little harder to handle.
There are many things I wish I could still do or be.
Life is very different now and those changes must be grieved.
Grieving the loss of something like that is inexplicable.
Losing a part of yourself is a different kind of mourning.

So I hope as you read this, you'll think a little more about how you can help.
Many people struggle with silent battles every day, and I want to show up for them.
If you have a loved one like me, please give them your empathy, your love, and your kindness.
We need all that we can get.

I AM WOMAN

First, they make you feel ugly.
Then, they make you feel fat.
Next, they make you feel insignificant.
Next, they make you feel insecure.
Finally, they make you feel unworthy.
So when you looked at my photos, you said make her arms smaller. Shrink them.
Then, you said my hair wasn't blonde enough. Brighten it.
Next, you said my boobs weren't big enough. Make them bigger.
Finally, you said to hide my freckles. Make them disappear.
The real problem here isn't me or being able to take that feedback because I really don't care. I do care that there are millions of little girls who think they should. The little girls who struggle with their weight and society says that it's okay that they get bullied. Bullied because there is this standard of ultimate beauty: an irresistible blonde girl, with skinny arms, big boobs and no flaws on her face, and apparently this doesn't quite meet the cut.
This is why little girls grow up thinking that they're ugly. This is why little girls grow up feeling like they're fat. This is why little girls grow up feeling insignificant, insecure, and unworthy.
But it gets worse.
This is why little girls grow to hate themselves. This is why little girls bully other little girls. This is why little girls hurt themselves. This is why little girls kill themselves.
So please, tell me I'm not all of these things. But don't you dare keep saying that to the little girls. This vicious standard is ludicrous. All women are beautiful in their own ways. There is no standard you can hold us all to. Little girls deserve real, authentic role models and women that go beyond this superficial facade. We are diverse. We are strong. We will lift each other while you keep tearing us down. I guarantee there is a little girl out there who needs you. Maybe it's your little sister, your best friend, or your daughter. Maybe it's your

niece, cousin, or significant other. The only way to stop the hurt and the pain is to stop accepting the old and demand a more inclusive standard of beauty. It doesn't matter how short or tall you are. It doesn't matter what color your skin is or how many freckles or scars you have. We are all beautiful, and together we can all stop this once and for all. Who is with me? No more body shaming.

TOGETHER

And when I say I'm on fire from head to toe.
Just because you can't see or feel it doesn't mean I can't feel the burn.
For there are times I wish the fire would die,
But perhaps I am meant to burn to keep my light shining.
A beacon in the darkness for those who lose hope,
Know that I burn with you, too; together we can cope.
I can't see your fire and I know you can't see mine,
But this is just a moment, frozen in time.
The pain can go on for days and days and days
And no matter how many things we try it just won't go away.
All I can do is share that you are not alone.
I'm here with you forever and then forevermore.
For maybe we burn so we can light the sky,
A star, a moon, a planet, a heavenly body Divine.
You are not alone, I am here to stay,
Together we can make it, moment by moment, day by day.
Feel my fire, feel my warmth, feel my hope, feel my love.
Together we burn and shine forever from the skies above.
This light is needed to guide others as we go,
The more we shine together, the stronger we will grow.

THE BLACK SHEEP

It feels like darkness, a foggy mind
That is never letting up.
There are some mornings where I think
What is the point of getting up?
It never made much sense to me why getting older was so great.
Now I worry about everything,
How much to give and what to take.
I don't sleep much anymore,
I barely ever dream.
I long for any normalcy at all
I don't even know what that means.
I don't understand
How everything went so wrong.
I really just wanted respect,
But now everything is gone.
No more family dinners,
No more Christmas trees.
At the end of it all
I just wanted to be free.
You hands around my neck so tight,
I forgot how to breathe.
Everyone can paint a picture,
See things that just aren't real.
You think I remember a childhood
Where did I learn to talk and how to feel?
I'm just a gray rock.
I've minimized, I've disengaged
I made myself even smaller trying to not be enraged.
30 years, 10950 days,
You've made it this far.
Just because the past may hurt,
It doesn't define who you are.

You may have learned a lesson,
Maybe even nine hundred and ninety-nine.
Just because it hurts your soul,
The sun will always shine.
Even if you can't find it,
Beyond the clouds and rain.
There will always be a light trying to keep us sane.
Maybe a star, maybe a moon, hurry up and make a wish.
It's time to accept the past, there is more to life than this.
Burn a book, turn the page,
But please don't let me go.
For I only know love like this,
Is it too late for me to grow?
I killed myself trying to not be a disgrace
To not bring shame upon the name.
I can't fit into a mold I never belonged
I'm the odd one out and I won't play the game.
Not anymore, no more "stranger danger".
I didn't run away, I found shelter
From the blows, the thunder, and the lightning.
I won't give into the philosophy of a Helter Skelter.
You're not the ruler of a kingdom,
There's not really anything to inherit on this earth to make me proud.
I'm okay now, and that's what really matters at the end of the day.
And it's time to be loud.

Rise up, black sheep,
But that's not what we are today.
We are lions, we are dragons,
No more damsels with dismay.
Letting go of baggage sometimes means people too.
It's not easy to accept that when humans aren't meant to be alone.
Remember who you are.
Rising up does not mean your heart is made of stone.
Each step will get easier, just start with one.

Your purpose is greater than pleasing the people who think they own you.
The thing about black sheep is that they're rare.
So this suffering is an opportunity that wasn't out of the blue.
The Bible says black sheep are worthless,
It's time for the outcasts to fight back and reclaim.
We're not going anywhere and we're not going to apologize.
We no longer live with the blame.
We're not here to make friends,
We're not here to make nice.
I'm no longer ashamed because my purpose is clear:
Less sugar, more spice.
People are uncomfortable when the black sheep is around,
They used to say hello, now they whisper behind us as we pass,
They won't understand until they see the power of standing out,
Buckle up now, it's time to hit the gas.

THE BEST FRIEND

May 12th 2006

You are the sunshine of my life,
Through the many perils, you help me survive.
Through all that is hard, all that is mundane,
Through all the tumultuous pain.
I can make it through,
But only with you by my side.
I've never known such things before,
As trust and pain and love,
But I'll never forget what you've helped me through,
Or what you helped me leave behind.
You are truly my best friend.
Without you the miles would have lasted forever,
The truths I fight for would never be reached,
And fear would never reach my mind.
You have truly blessed my life,
And blessed me as who I am.
What a special human you are,
That helps me through these days.
Mountains become plains,
And rain becomes shine,
And laughter never sounded so perfect,
As the person whom I call my best friend.

RUN

Dear sister, there is always time to leave your old self behind,
Let us walk together and keep the following in mind:
It's waking up everyday trying to be better than the day before.
It's crossing goals off your list and then adding even more.
It's having goals to believe in, that is where it all begins,
Sometimes the hardest thing is to listen to the voice within.
There comes a time where we have to stop worrying about the rest of the world,
We must take a stand and be a hero, the one you needed when you were a little girl.
The one who was supposed to tell how hard it all would be,
The one who was supposed to make her believe in her own dreams.
Instead, she got lost, like many other little girls do,
She kept making wishes and dreaming things that would never come true.
She wished to win the lotto so her parents never worried about money again,
She wished that her friends cared about her as much as she cared about them.
She was afraid of getting in trouble, the anger and the wrath,
She would hide and cry in her room, trying to find her own path.
It went on like this for years, never understanding what she did wrong,
All she wanted was a voice and to feel like she would belong.
She worried about getting anything less than an "A."
She didn't want the monster to come out again today.
She lived in toxic walls that could only be found,
By the ones who suffered inside and were afraid to make a sound.
The words, the anger, the abuse, the rage,
But the scars were never visible, even though she was in a cage.
The house that I grew up in was never was a home,
It was a place with walls and beds, not a place to enjoy life and roam.
There were days of happiness, there were days of joy.
There were days of music and dancing and Santa bringing toys.

But just like Maya says, it's not what they did or what they said,
It's how it made you feel in your heart, your soul, and your head.

You will never forget the damage, the destruction and the despair.
How you were never taught the simple things like how to brush your hair.
You will never forget how your pillow was your favorite thing,
Because it gave you comfort, something no one else in the house could bring.
Something you could hold while you cried your tears,
Something that could protect you from your mind's biggest fears.
Anything to give you peace, a pillow, a doll, a bed,
From all the evil spirits swirling around in and outside your head.
Even your room wasn't safe, she would go through all the trash,
It was like you were never trusted and living with a psychopath.
You were never worthy, you were never good.
You were just a nuisance and you were never understood.
How to fix it, how to make it end,
She never taught you on purpose, so she could complain about it again.
It was a never ending cycle, vicious to say the least.
No Beauty to be found, just a vicious Beast.
Hurry now child, you must leave this all behind,
Protect your heart, protect your soul, and most of all, your mind.
You are not like her and will never be.
You must convince yourself of this or you'll never be free.
Run from this, my child, and never look back,
For the road ahead is better, and you must stay on track.
Even though it hurts and you're afraid of what they will say,
It's better to be free than trapped in a cave for another day.
You must run, you must walk, and maybe even crawl ahead,
Leave that little girl behind now and all the dread,
Your heart and your soul have bled,
Goodbye to the past, for now it is dead.

LOOKING UP

At what age does a child no longer get to be one? Is it 16? Is it 18? It is an age? Or is it an experience? Is it feeling pain for the first time? Loss of a loved one? Is it being injured?
We all have defining moments. Either the moment defines us by our action, reaction, or lack thereof, or we define ourselves.
Are we cowards, or are we brave?
Can we stand up for ourselves?
Are our voices strong enough?
It's hard to explain my pain or that I feel betrayed.
It's hard to write this down because seeing it in writing makes it even more real, and I have to feel.
I feel the anger, the hurt, and the burden of being here because that is what you wanted.
Isn't it wild that the greatest heartbreak of all is because your guardians couldn't let go and let you breathe on your own?
Being under a toxic cloud for so long, I didn't know one could be so sick.
The poison was so thick and when I found where the sky kissed freedom,
And was strong enough to breathe in pure clean air for the first time,
I realized that I died a long time ago, and I didn't know that being alive could be such a lie.
I was reborn the day I finally crossed the horizon and found a line,
That little girl had to be left behind.
The weight of her was why it took me so long to learn how to fly.
I live for her now, and I'm never looking back, only ahead is my sky.

THE BEST FRIEND PART DEUX

An empty page, an empty stage
I'm always feeling lost.
I thought I would know more by now,
Maybe life is but a bust.
I spend hours thinking,
But no words come out on paper.
I know my time is running out,
I feel like I'm trying to climb a skyscraper.
This journey is not normal,
Unfair for a young girl.
The things I have seen and been forced to live through,
While trying to make it in the world.
Maybe the choices of the past
Will leave the future unharmed.
The problem is I no longer feel safe
And feel like I should be armed.
Armed with words, armed with weapons,
We must stand our ground.
It seems I try to raise my voice,
But I can't make a sound.
Am I worthy? Am I brave?
Questions that always haunt a woman.
Maybe I'm not all that great,
After all, I'm only human.
I know I have seen more of evil than most other people do,
In a lifetime of growth and change,
We must search for our own breakthrough.
We must keep crawling forward even when we cannot stand,
I see you on the ground sister,
I'm here to help you up and hold your hand.
This was never about me or me trying to shine,
I maybe need your hand more than you will ever need mine.

For so long I thought I would go this road alone,
But the truth is I never was, even when I was grown.
Walk with me, by my side as you always will.
Even when you or I fall down, the other will be standing still.
It's okay if you can't catch me even when I fall,
I know I can count on you even if I run into a wall,

Hand in hand, side by side,
I promise to you tonight,
That I will keep going if you do too and we will never stop without a fight.
Promise me that you never want this to end,
Because at the end of the day you were always my best friend.

QUEEN OF THE COURT

There is something in me I have to prove.
There's a reason I'm here and it's not to lose.
I am the one I could be in my dreams.
I am a leader on all of my teams.
I will strive each day to be the best.
I refuse to lose against any test.
The only thing that matters is my dream.
I will push myself to reach it, no matter the cost.
My dream lives on forever until I achieve,
What I must have to become my life-long dream.
My dream pushes me to the limits and you can't take that away from me.
No matter what the sport, I will always be Queen of the Court.

Shay, age 15

THE GOOD SIR PART DEUX

I miss you.
I know you're here, but I wish for more.
You speak to me with the Blue Jay.
You leave white feathers around me to remind me I'm not alone.
I miss you.
We will be together again.
Thank you for sending him to me.
Thank you.

THE VILLAIN HERO

You might be a hero, but more often than not, you're a villain in someone else's story.

There should be moments of deep reflection before we label someone as this.

It shouldn't be a knee jerk reaction.

It shouldn't be a trigger.

Sometimes as humans, we make bad decisions.

The difference between a hero, a human, and a villain to me goes something like this:

A hero recognizes when they've hurt others, learns from their mistakes, and chooses to do better.

A human is a human- imperfect, flawed, but armed with the choice to do better or not.

A villain never does better, never chooses better, never becomes anything better.

So while we aspire to be heroes, there are days where being human will outshine that sparkle, but as long as we choose to do better, we are better.

The world makes us jaded, sad, and feel very small sometimes.

Choosing to be the villain does nothing for you except break your karma.

Maybe you'll get what you want faster, but that doesn't mean you won't pay in other ways.

The universe is a kind place for those who choose to find the beauty in their humanness.

Some people pay a heavy toll to just feel alive, never knowing the light within, if they were patient enough, would light the way.

The world requires balance, which is why we will always have heroes and villains, and being human is making the choice when we look in the mirror every morning whose team we are going to play on.

I know which team I want to play on.

HEY (INSERT NAME HERE)

Hey (Shay)
You didn't know better
You were just doing what you were told
It's okay
You did your best
That's all anyone can ever ask
So why do you punish yourself still
Isn't it time to live?
Thrive?
Believe again?

THE LAST STOP

"Hope is the only thing stronger than fear."
That's what they always say.
I wasn't always operational, but I was ready.
I wasn't always optimal, but I had fire.
I wasn't always ready for a fight, but I had soul.
I'm not sure when you compare me in the ring to another I would match up so well, but it didn't matter.
There was only one person who needed to enter the ring, and it was me.
And we are going home.
Resurgence isn't always a destination, but now, it is everything.

Resurgence

"You know that thing you want to do?
That thing you watch other people do.
That thing your heroes do.
Go do that.
But don't do it
like anyone else
has ever done before.
-Go your own way-
J.Warren Welch

DECLARATION OF INDEPENDENCE

I've let too many people walk all over me because I was afraid to use my voice.

You didn't show me how.

I was afraid to tell people "no" because you didn't show me how.

I was afraid of you because you made me afraid of you.

You ruled with fear, and the only person whose feelings mattered were yours.

Mine were always made to be nothing so I felt like I was nothing.

I was so afraid of getting into trouble, I was an angel on the outside, but on the inside I was a scared little girl trying to not forget to breathe.

The trauma response remained for years and years.

It wasn't until I was older and felt more empowered and brave that I tried to put boundaries in place.

Again, you didn't trust, respect, or communicate with me in a healthy manner.

You verbally destroyed me, what I do for a living, my accomplishments, and everything I would ever be proud of.

So no, you don't get to keep gaslighting me with your poisonous words and empty promises.

You don't get to tell me who I am or what to do.

Not anymore.

This is my Declaration of Independence for me and all the other little girls.

The little girls who got left behind and had to find their own way, new definitions of home, all the while screaming silently, internally at the injustices while presenting a smile on their faces to the world.

Stop telling us to smile when you have no idea what we've survived.

GLIMMER

Angel numbers and butterflies find me everyday now.
111 tells me to trust myself and listen to my intuition.
222 tells me I'm aligned, I'm in the right place, the right time.
333 tells me I'm supported, loved and being guided.
444 tells me I'm protected by my guides and the universe.
555 tells me something new this way comes.
I'm a little bit scared, I'm a little bit impatient.
I've been waiting my whole life for this moment.
I flow now, where before I fought, froze, or fled.
I flow now because I trust.
I flow now because I'm aligned.
I flow now because I'm held.
I flow now because I'm protected.
I flow now because I'm ready.
My friend said "amazing awaits".
Ever since I heard the phrase, it gave me hope.
It gave me a path.
It gave me the belief that I could have more than what I had.
That I could be more than what I was.
I'm not sure I will ever be fully satisfied, but when I wake up, I know I flow.
Synchronicity is not a coincidence.
You're here for a reason, just like all these signs.
On days we need reminders, these numbers call to us.
On days we struggle, a butterfly flies by to remind you,
Hope, change, transformation, positivity,
There was a time the beautiful butterfly was a cocoon, making a decision in the darkness if they wanted to find the light.
Every day we make decisions to either move forwards or backwards,
To stay in the shell or leave it to find the light.
Sometimes we are blind to what the shell is,
Sometimes we miss the lessons in the darkness,

May you embrace knowing there will be so many versions of you born,
That you never fear the dark again, dear one.
One cocoon at a time.
One beautiful butterfly at a time.
Fly away with me.

NEVER

Never give up a broken dream, for nothing is beyond repair.
Never forsake words of wisdom when in a state of despair.
Forgive all those you love before it is too late.
Always cherish those you love, and always give your thanks.
Never forget a golden moment, for few they seem to be.
Never give into temptation or pressure,
Keep your choices free.
Remember those who changed your life,
When love and trust were few,
Never blow out the candle of hope when no one has a clue.
Believe in the impossible when dreams begin to fade.
Dreams and hope are always there and never put to trade.
So dream and love and remember all those who help you on your way,
to the path where life leads you to until your dying day.

BEST

I've never had a friend as close to me as you,
We had many struggles and you always helped me through.
When I've fallen, you've helped me to my feet,
When stress and hardships came along you refused to call defeat.
You've been there for me, firmly at my side.
You've given me the confidence and will to fight the demons inside.
Best friends forever and no matter how far apart,
I'll always be there for you, the sister in my heart.

HOPE

I hope you find peace.
I hope you find hope.
I hope you find strength
And new ways to cope.
I hope there is light.
I hope there is love.
For all of those days
You couldn't look above.
I hope you find shelter
From the cruelty and the cold.
I hope you find your voice
To speak up and be bold.
Though I may not be there
The way I was before.
I implore you to look within
And ask yourself for more.
For the days will go on
And the years will fly by.
Did you do all you wished for?
Did you really try?
Time is the only thing we have
To make up for the loss and all that is bad.
We may never regain what was before
So I ask again, "Don't you want more?"
And if you decide there is no more to be done,
Then don't you dare hold me back
I've only just begun.
So fitting.
When I spread my wings and rise again from the ashes,
I will never be more glorious.

THE MENTOR

It's already October of another year and I feel like I wasted another opportunity to do something with my life. I ask my mentor to call me because I'm feeling broken, again.

He said, "No one gets to determine your self-confidence or self-worth. Only you."

And then he asked me the hardest question of my life. "Do you believe you are worthy?"

My answer was weak and triggered trauma, so I stumbled through words. I never felt worthy as a child, and still those claws hold a tight grip on my skin and poison my mind.

After a short cry, I knew I couldn't do this anymore. I couldn't be this version of myself anymore. The internal battle between the light and darkness inside me came to an abrupt halt. I said out loud the introduction for myself that I was preparing for a program in the mirror. At thirty years old, I should be very proud. I should be more than proud. I should be beaming. Finally, at thirty years old, I was able to crown myself as worthy.

It's October 12th. This was the day I knew I had to change my life. Too many years of trauma triggering feelings of unworthiness. The vicious cycle had to be broken and the only way to end it was to feel completely and utterly in control of my life. If I fail, I fail. If I succeed, I succeed. Nothing more and nothing less. No more excuses. I get to control my destiny. I work hard. I am good at what I do. I am smart. I am capable. And I am so very worthy. It does not matter what the rest of the world thinks. I am the one who will be the judge of that. Everything else is a waste of my time.

WE

My dearest one.
My pride and joy.
My sweet, innocent inner child.
There was a time you sang and danced fearlessly.
But then the monster came, so you only felt safe in your room.
You were safe there in the quiet with your headphones on, living in a world disassociating yourself so you could find freedom from your reality.
The stories, the songs, the other lives you wanted to live–that was the only way for you to stay sane.
I'm sorry no one spoke up for you.
I'm sorry no one stood up for you.
I'm sorry you never saw how it took you so long to learn how to do it yourself.
I'm sorry you worked so hard to be perfect, but then were told you never did anything right.
I'm sorry for how fast you had to grow up.
I'm sorry you didn't have a real childhood.
I'm sorry they broke your heart.
And even though the journey hasn't been easy, it has been meaningful.
Your dark night of the soul was not in vain.
You were a star in the dark sky waiting to burst, to shine, to give light.
You are light, the purest white to grace the sky.
You are and always were a good, decent human being, with a beautiful soul.
I am so proud of you.
I am so grateful that you never gave up.
I am still here living and breathing because of you.
We are not one without the other.
A house is not a home without you by my side, dear one.
I love you. I love you. I love you.
The greatest love of all will always be you.

Beautiful, sweet, dear little girl, we made it.
We are home. We are love. We are light.
We are one. We are healed. We are safe.
My dearest one, we found our way back to each other.
My dearest one, we have arrived.

CHOICE

I hope that there is a day, a moment, a time
Where you realize that everything led to where you are.
You remember when you didn't think you could keep going, but you did.
You made a decision that was pivotal without knowing how far you would come.
That is the moment of rebirth.
That is the moment you claim your place in this world.
For we are phoenixes who rise over and over again.
We are the children of the universe who have decided our mark on this earth will not be defined by days, moments in time.
We are defined by the choices to never give up, regardless of how many spectators are cheering in the stands of our life.
Your biggest fan must always be you.
No else can can understand that being a champion doesn't always mean a medal around your neck,
It's the choice to keep going, despite the odds that separate us from the rest.
Burn with me and rise again.

EMPIRE

And when the stars finally aligned, the universe lost its patience.
The time came to finally move on from the past onto bigger and better things.
Maybe everything does happen for a reason.
The past had to hurt so her voice could be found.
The bridges had to burn so she could learn how to walk alone until her true tribe was found.
She had to fall over and over again, not to learn how to walk.
She had to find her wings and fly.
When she finally saw the vision of what she deserved, she knew it was time.
It was time to let go.
Every step builds off the one before it.
Every breath brings you close to the summit, you can feel it now.
You've given everything for this, running low on nothing but faith in yourself.
The blood, the sweat, the tears, they've allowed you to build your foundation.
Now, it's your time.
Build your empire and never look back.

BURN

She was ice and fire. A Phoenix taking flight for the last time. Each time the fire burned more, until she reached the point of no return. The point where the fire must go out to be reborn again. There is beauty in pain. There is beauty in leaving this life for another. Wait for me there, when the world ends, I want to burn with only you.

7-7-07

Today is the luckiest day in a thousand years,
So I'll put that luck to the test.
I have dreams inside my head
That may be big, but that does NOT mean unreachable.
So today I'll make my vow,
To strive to become the woman in my dreams,
I'll fight and refuse to acknowledge failure,
I'll remove it from my vocabulary.
And I will never give up,
No matter what people think or believe,
And I WILL prove them all wrong.
I will become who I was meant to be,
No matter what it takes.

YOUR PERSON

Your person feels like home.
It doesn't matter where you are, you feel safe.
You trust in him.
Not all the flags are green, but there are more green than red.
The love is unspoken.
You just know.
Your inner child is smiling.
You both feel safe, happy, and loved.
You believe in magic again.
You believe in love again.
You are home.

WHOLE

October 26th, 2021

I am free.
I am released from all burdens, all expectations, all heaviness.
Anything and everything that adds weight to my mind, my heart, and soul.
I am a child of the universe built in love and light.
My soul is light and free and full of purpose.
From now on, in this human experience, I release the unfair weight of the world.
I force this upon myself because I feel I must provide the worthiness of my existence at my own expense.
I wasn't taught how to function, or live, or even how to breathe properly.
The weight in my chest and heaviness on my heart is not my own.
It comes from a long time ago when my heart was shattered.
It was many lives ago, but the trauma has carried onto this life.
I cannot carry this anymore.
This human experience was the one to break the generational curse.
The one I've failed to release myself from over and over.
The universe calls me to a greater purpose this time- in order to move forward, I must let go of the past that drags me down.
Former me forgives you for not catching on sooner.
Former me releases how hard it can be to move on.
Former me is grateful for those lessons and experiences who shaped me to be the version of myself today.
But this me wants more- to find the highest version of myself.
To fulfill the purpose of my soul.
So I ask the angels, spirit guides, Mother Earth, and Father God- my dear universe,
I am ready to move on.
I am ready to let go.

I am ready to forgive.
I forgive all past versions of myself for any failings, trauma, and curses that still affect me today.
I am grateful to them for showing me the way.
I forgive myself for anything I've done that brings me shame, guilt, sadness, and fear.
I let go of anything and everything that no longer serves my highest good.
I break free from the past.
I am worthy of moving forward to find my highest self.
My inner child-I love you. Be with me now.
Everything I do is to protect you and find ways to give you the love you always deserved.
Together, we walk like warriors across this field together, hand in hand, side by side- we move forward.
The past is done and over.
We will focus more on the present and enjoy life more.
We are open to love and the divine messages of the universe.
The journey has not been easy, but the reward of what lies ahead will bring us peace.
For we are whole now.
So be it, so it is.

LOVE

11/04/2004

If I could tell the world one thing, it would be to stop and listen to every voice and see what they have to say. But some of us won't-too busy, too ignorant, too arrogant. But if that one voice made a difference in the way you view the world, one sentence to tell the world, even one word can make a change. From war to peace, from hate to love, from chaos to harmony. If I could say one sentence to the world it would be "Why do you ignore someone who has something to say?" But if I could only get one word- "love." Love everyone the way you love yourself. Love yourself as you love the world. The world is so big and you are so small. Change the world so you can stand on top of it and be the person you were meant to be. You are better than you think you are.

FLYING

Now we're flying, living our best lives, free of everything that held us back.
We are grateful for the adversity because it made us strong.
Finally breathing without the weight of the world in our chests,
Released from the burdens of the past, we may not be able to run like we could when we were young,
But we learned to walk again.
We learned that putting one foot in front of the other was progress-
Even if it was slow, it was still moving forward, and this was progress,
This was winning.
This is the momentum needed to move on beyond the pain,
All the days that were too much, the suffering of yesterday,
That is where those memories live now.
There are no more flashbacks, uncontrolled triggers, moments of doubt, or questions of self.
We are whole, we are healed, we are divine.
Our aura is strong, yet gentle enough to embrace letting go of the armor we once carried around our heart.
We have more faith now, we believe a little more now,
and we lead with love, grace and hope- fear no longer holds us back.
Instead we channel those feelings with grace.
We no longer live in fear- we live FREE.

HEY WORLD

Hey world, look at me.
I'm flying, soaring through clouds of white.
I need to reach my home.
I need to find my place.
I need to escape from the dungeons of my mind,
The beliefs of the world.
The pieces of my dreams.
They are lost in the jungles of the world.
Oh, they're lost- lost to the innocent, searching for the angels.
Angels, hear my call.
Calling all the world to listen - listen to my voice that once spoke with despair.
Don't assume I'm hopeful by rambling on and on.
Wishing for my purpose, wishing for the signs of truth.
Their lies are demeaning, their lies are cruel.
They make you believe you're worth something more than life.
Wake up mother nature, wake up quietude.
Wake up friends and families, before they're gone.
Don't fall for cunning lies, don't listen to what they say.
Stay away from curses and never go away.
Peace is crumbling fast, crumbling like a wall that once stood tall,
Falling like a feather, that falls ever so slow.
They made me mad and crazy,
They drive me up a wall.
Patience is going fast, losing all its might.
My words are losing sense- sense and all its pride.
Never ceasing, never going.
Going like the words of something more than life itself.
Peace is not what I thought it would be,
But my words are stronger than ever,
When I realized my words are everlasting,
and will go on despite all this.

THE TEACHER

While many people have crossed my path, not everyone has the privilege to stay.
For a long time I thought they did because I felt so little.
But people along the way saw me
When I didn't see myself.
People believed I had more to give the world than I could imagine.
So when I understood that the people were the magic,
I mean they are the ones who help paint a picture of a world where you are meant to be.
He said, "Brilla, mi Estrella"
And I said I'll never stop burning bright.
He never saw what was broken
He just saw the gold keeping it all together.

And when I forgot what a beautiful piece of art it all was,
He made sure I remembered.
So many versions of both of us have come and gone,
But the love is the same.
Because I'll never forget that good people are the ones who make you feel alive
Some of my best memories will always be with you
Thank you for reminding me that I was always the light
I hope to keep shining a path so you always find home
And know I'm always with you in all space and time,
In all lives, for together we make the world a better place
At least I know I am a better person waking up each morning knowing you still exist
It's hard to put into words what "Brilla, mi Estrella" did for me,
Or even the fact that you knew so many years ago that I was light in my darkness,
And you never left.
You were meant to be my star too.
For we all need to know we will never walk this world alone.
When one star is struggling, another burns brighter.
Thank you for being more than just a star.
You are a goddamn supernova in a world that puts people's fires out without blinking.
And how you share that light without ever wanting anything in return.
It's a selfless act to be a teacher.
It's a selfless act to be a good human too.
My god, the world could use so many more of you,
But how lucky am I to have found a human supernova?
I always loved that "maestro" was a teacher in Spanish, because of course it was.
You are leading so many orchestras, I'm just here to watch.

THE HEALER PART DEUX

She took me by the hand
She fought by my side
These battles I couldn't fight myself
She gave me the messages I needed to hear
And when push came to shove
When the energy was so stagnant
She never gave up on me
And the magic was her.

And she helped me remember
Who I really was
And even after all this time
It was never really about healing
It was about finding the power and voice within
It was always there
Buried beneath the trauma and the grief
Every three days for three months
Until I finally found my wings
And then the magic was me
Miracles are extraordinary, surprising
How else can you explain this?
They said I wouldn't be able to and yet, I was able to.
How do you thank someone who helped to save your life?
By passing it on and shining the light.
So others believe in their magic again too.

PERFECTLY IMPERFECT

Somewhere the fearless one who raised her hand with confidence lost her way.
She started panicking when called on because she didn't want to be exposed.
Exposed for what, you might ask?
It's normal as a human to be wrong.
It's not normal for a perfectionist.
We hold ourselves to impossible standards and wonder why the rest of the world does not.
And it's exhausting.
So much so that I'm burnt out from my existence on the planet.
We live in fear that people will stop loving us or there are dire consequences for breathing wrong.
So I wrote this book and stopped before I thought it was perfect.
Now I know, it never will be whatever that definition means.
It just needs to be enough for me.
To release the words that have infested my body for over three decades.
I can't carry them anymore.
For now, I'm a recovering perfectionist.
And that's okay.

THE SAFE ONE

My person loves me for everything I am- the good, the bad, and everything in between.

He is kind to me when I'm not my best self because he knows I'm trying my best.

On days I am not feeling well, he encourages and supports me by never leaving my side.

On days I am top of the world, he is so proud to call me their partner.

And all the other days, he enjoys the peace of my comfort, as our time together is the best gift we can give one another.

And when we are together, the world is a better place.

He has my heart and gives me theirs without demands.
Sometimes you don't realize the darkness until you find their light leading you home.
I believe the words coming out of his mouth.
Once the veil is lifted, everything feels natural and easy.
Together we can rule the world, the galaxy, the universe, hand in hand.
One day you wake up and you know this is who you want to wake up next to every day for the rest of your days.
He says my scars don't make me any less beautiful.
He wants me to be happy and comfortable.
And then he tells you he loves you.
But he never had to say the words.
You already knew.
And if that wasn't enough,
The voices are screaming at me,
That I'll never be alone again.
So then I tell him:
"You were always my home.
And I was so tired making this journey,
But there you were.
I'm not sure if I was broken, unhealed, or incomplete,
But I never wanted to make someone else feel any of those things,
And I knew what I wanted,
So I put myself back together,
And I told the universe I wanted you,
And there you were.
Maybe it felt like the wait was so long,
But it was worth it."
For he was the sunshine I always needed
And I never wanted to melt more in my life.
Everything feels safe.
Everything feels so easy.
Does this scare me? Yes.
But this time is different.
I see only green flags ahead.

I still hold my breath sometimes.
I'm still afraid you might leave,
But my nervous system says
"You don't live there anymore."
"This is home."

THE SISTER

In the beginning, the Evil Queen never wanted peace, she wanted division.

So we were a divided house, never understanding that we were supposed to all be on the same team from the get go.

She made me not like her because I was told she was a problem, a diva, a princess.

And I was not- I was an Angel, Miss Cellophane, a tomboy.

Years passed and I never realized my greatest ally slept in the same room as me for most of my life.

It wasn't until she was no longer there, I realized the people in power made me believe the opposite of the truth.

She may be a princess, but without a mentor or a role model, I didn't know how to be an adult.

I was never told or taught how to do so many things, but she never left me behind.

And when the day came I realized how unfair it all was, I was mortified about how wrong I was about the one person who really loved me.

And when I was ready to accept everything that I allowed to happen, the decisions made for me not with me, and the person I wanted to be, I stood up to the Evil Queen.

I said I needed to be addressed directly, I said healthy relationships are two way streets and that any conflicts I had with others, I could handle myself.

These words were twisted from healthy boundaries to making me an exiled black sheep, but I was not going to tolerate this childish behavior anymore.

When we are faced with choices, we don't always want to choose the difficult path.

There are times in life where going left isn't fair and neither is going right.

We can only do the best we can.

I've never been more proud than watching her break the cycle.
Raising her children not the way we were.
Creating a safe space that we deserved but never had.
Giving love selflessly, without expectations, simply meeting expectations of the choice of being a parent.
You see a lot of people build resentment from a place of what they think they deserve,
But nobody in this life is entitled to a damn thing,
However, a parent should be expected to provide the bare minimum to love.
To care, to champion, to nurture, to teach, to provide, to try to make their little version into a decent human being.
One that is empowered to believe in the beauty of their dreams, and not punished for breathing in the same walls that the parent is expected to keep safe and standing.
There are three little good humans walking this earth now.
I'm sure one will rule the world, one will teach love, and one will create beauty- for these things define them, and how she lets them thrive.
I often think about how if I were them, how different my life would be.
It makes me smile to see them thrive from a very young age, but I'm not bitter or resentful, I'm happy, I'm blessed, I am loved now more than I could ever imagine.
Because she decided to make her own family and made sure she didn't leave me behind.

I knew she never would, we both needed some time to find our way to this pathway of healing.
There are so many things along the way that didn't go right or well, but I never doubted for a moment that it would end up any other way.
There are many soulmates in our lives, but this one is more than that.
To encapsulate all the roles isn't fair either, so I will simply say she is my person.
To say more or less is just not enough, for the words aren't tangible.
But you see it in the way she carries herself, how much love she is given, how people gravitate towards her.
In a world where people are afraid to be themselves, what a beautiful thing to see-
A radiant cyclebreaker, who smiles now at the world where she found the path to be better, and did.
The cycle stops here, dear one.
The cycle stopped here.

She found her "HER".
My dear sister.
The cyclebreaker.
The world is a better place because you were so brave.
The world is a better place with you in it.
In a lineage with rows of burnt matches, you didn't burn–you skipped a row, and now those gentle ripples of waves carry on your legacy.
And their mighty waves roar all thanks to you.
They don't give medals for breaking cycles because the impact isn't understood until it's personal,
But I know if there was one, it would be gold.
So I honor that legacy by knowing better, choosing better, and believing that we are making the world a little bit better than it was than when we were the three growing up and trying to find our way.
We come with lanterns and lights, we come with ropes and life jackets, because we will never let anything happen to them like it did to us.
Not out of spite, or resentment, but simply because there should be no other way.
They say there are two kinds of people in the world- one that believes in not helping and that people have to learn the hard way, and the other, who will do everything in their power to make other people's lives a little bit easier.
We know we were blessed with light for a reason.
You can still teach and show the path to the next generation.
You can still give love even when it's tough.
It's never "You think you had it bad, you have no idea."
It's always "Here's my hand and if you need it, I will walk with you forever."
Cyclebreakers are superheroes who look like normal people, but there is nothing average about them at all.
What an honor it is to walk amongst warriors.
What an honor it is to witness rising above.
What an honor it is to know we did this together.
We did it.
Thank you.
My seester.

RESILIENCE

Resilience- the ability to withstand adversity and bounce back from difficult life events
It doesn't mean that everyday is easy now.
It doesn't mean that you aren't allowed to show emotions.
It means that you survived.
It means that you endured.
It means that trauma and grief no longer define your day to day spirit.
It means you were able to recover.
It means you found the light in the darkness.
It means you learned how to get up.
That you refused to be stuck any longer.
You lifted yourself from rock bottom.
You recognize your worth and that you deserve happiness and joy and love.
All of the good that you once believed you didn't deserve.
You pulled yourself back to the starting line, so you could begin again.
You should be so proud.
It wasn't easy, picking yourself back up over and over again.
But you are here where YOU decide who you are now.
There was nothing that was going to hold you back anymore.
You've decided you deserve better.
You were always so much more.

You are brave.
You endured.
You are a survivor.
You are a warrior.
You are everything.
You are endless.
You are light.
You are love.
You are RESILIENT.

A LETTER FOR YOUR BIRTHDAY

Happy birthday, baby girl! Today is your birthday. It is hard to believe how quickly the years pass by, yet some days live on forever. Some memories will never fade, some joys will never go away. Today, we celebrate the woman you have become. The successes and triumphs have equally shaped you as the pain and the horrors. No one has lived your life or is entitled to you and all that you are. You have earned your place in the world. You earned this every day you didn't give up despite the pain. You earned this when you found your voice and the strength within. You earned this by choosing to live despite the darkness, and looking for the stars when the night was so dark.

Your strengths are your fire, your calm in the face of the storm, and your undying passion to make the world a better place. You never had a female role model to look up to. A strong female warrior who stands for what is right, even when it is hard. You realized you weren't going to find that hero or mentor, so you became her instead.

You are your own Wonder Woman. You are unwavering and unstoppable. You must never give up because this is not just for you. This is for the other little girls who needed someone to help them, someone to stand up for them, and someone to believe in them. Be the person you needed when you were younger. Be your own superhero. You are your own star. Never let someone else dim your light-for someone else may need to follow it to find their own star in the sky.

Wonder Woman says, "I will fight for those who cannot fight for themselves." Wonder Woman also says, "Now I know that only love can truly save the world, so I stay, I fight, and I give- for the world that I know can be." I promise to continue to fight, to love, and give to you, little one. I promise to be your own Wonder Woman, so hopefully another little girl doesn't feel your pain.

SORRY MASLOW

I think if I've learned anything in this life, it's that it's very hard to figure things out on your own. There is a comfort that showing someone how to do something for the first time truly provides. The psychological safety around it being okay if you fail because someone is there beside you to show the way. Unfortunately, having ultra independence is no longer something I view as a strength, although something perhaps others have admired about me. In the end, I think it's much, much braver now to ask for help.

No one person can do everything. To pretend otherwise is just not acknowledging our limitations as human beings. We rarely celebrate the times in our humanity where we fail and learn and do better. The celebrations stop at some grand achievement. It's really all about the journey. The steps you chose to keep climbing despite the struggles. The belief that you can keep going, despite the odds. People won't remember that you weren't perfect or that you asked for help along the way. They will remember how you treated them when you were struggling and not quite at the finish line yet. While the perfectionist, overachieving Shay certainly got me this far, it has come with great costs. Some at the expense of others- right, wrong, or indifferent. I used to think I could outwork anyone and I did for a long time because I knew I was never the smartest person in the room. I just worked really hard.

But then I remember the love of being on a team where you work as a unit, know each other's strengths and weaknesses, and find the right combination to be something greater than one person. Our egos tell us we must outshine everyone else to be happy, but the joy was always the community and shared purpose and growth. Having a safe place to land when things got tough.

I don't miss the days of winning an award or getting my next promotion, I miss the shared passion and mission where I stood shoulder to shoulder with people that wanted to win just as badly as I did. I certainly still want to be a winner, but I would rather be a good team player, part of something greater than one shining star that will go out eventually because they spent all their energy trying to be seen by a world that is "pay to play". Some people will never be seen for who they are because the world isn't looking for the right things. Everyone has a different definition of what success and happiness look like. Whatever that is, I hope you find it with the people who never gave up on you. I hope you know that you're not alone when the days are much harder than others.

Pride and ego are the death of self-actualization. You'll never find it if you think you're already the best version of yourself. Sorry Maslow, I said what I said.

READY

I hope my soul can find peace.
I hope my peace brings others hope.
I hope that those who need it will listen.
I will listen to my spirit guides so I can find my way home.
I'm ready to heal and move on.
I'm ready for my next chapter.
I'm ready to let go and begin again.
For all that is meant to be, will be, and I hope when the time comes, all is well with my soul.

ALL IS WELL

On the days I feel like I'm burning alive, you stay by my side and burn with me.
You may not see the flames, but you feel the heat.
For that I struggle to find the right words to say that without you my world wouldn't keep turning.
And should the day come my fire consumes me, I'll never see darkness.
For your light is always there to guide me home.
A light that only burns enough to guide me to a place I can leave this all behind.
I'll wait for you there, for only with you all is well with my soul.

THE PURGE

There is no magic wand that makes trauma go away.
There is no spell strong enough to make me forget what you did to me.
At first I thought it would be easier if I could, but I can't forget. I can't let it go.
For without the trauma and overwhelming obsession of me, I would have never learned how to love someone else truly and unconditionally.
I had to feel the horror of being loved as an object that could be controlled by fear and terror.
I had to be afraid of what the next day would bring.
Otherwise, I would have never found peace in the chaos of my childhood.
I am no object that can be controlled.
I am free from your spells and chokehold.
You don't own me.
For I remember and always will the day you decided that power was more important than a child's innocent request.
I knew when you stopped saying you loved me that you didn't ever mean it in the first place.
It was all just part of the spell you had over me, controlling all I've ever known.
Now it's just a word that means nothing to me as you never really loved me anyway.
This is the last poem I'm wasting on you.

THE EAGLE MUST BURN

The Phoenix watched from afar as the Eagle arrogantly raised his beak from his perch far above the rest of the land. It was a proud beast. Perhaps, too proud. It guarded the nest he built with almost as much fire as a Phoenix.

The Eagle was smart, but it made a fatal mistake. It believed that being an Eagle was more important than the lives of the other animals in the land beneath him. The fish that provide food for other animals, the butterflies that are born from a cocoon, and the bees that help give us beautiful flowers … the Eagle cared nothing for these tasks as these animals were beneath him, just like the work they take the most pride in.

The Eagle was so blind to what he wanted, he didn't realize that without the fish and the butterflies and the bees, the land would die. If it wasn't for them, there would be nothing. The Eagle has never known what nothing is like, yet he is the harshest judge of those who have little compared to his bird's eye view.

The Phoenix sees the world. The Phoenix sees the whole picture. The Phoenix understands that an Eagle can't speak for those who live in the real world beneath him. The world where most people are not Eagles.

The Phoenix never wants to be an Eagle. The Phoenix wants to lift up those who make the land a better place and don't get what they deserve because of animals like the Eagle. Even a fish and a bee deserve happiness, though they are small and perhaps not mighty. Even a butterfly deserves a chance to fly around the world. If this is to happen, the Eagle can't win. The Eagle can't speak for us. He must go down in flames. He must burn.

THEY KNOW THE COST

Sisters are different. They heard the sobbing in the darkness. They lived through all your triumphs, all your favorites, all your loves and losses. They have no delusions. They lived with you too long. And so, when you achieve some victory, friends are delighted - but sisters hold your hands in silence and shine with happiness. For they know the cost.

SURVIVAL GUIDE

It's important you share your stories. People may not "like" your status or comment or speak to you at all anymore, but they see you. If there's 100 haters out there, go ahead and let them hate. If your message can brighten someone's day, do it. If you overcame something, tell the world. This was never about being better than other people or showing off. It was meant to bring people together, to celebrate life, and connect us in a world that spins way too fast. The world is going to keep spinning with or without you, so tell your friends you love them. If you think of someone, message or call them. If someone opens up to you, listen and believe them. If someone is not responding, keep knocking on their door. If you can bring someone in the darkness back into the light, sit beside them until they're ready. The most powerful thing is to help someone believe they can make it because they know you did it. But if you don't share your story, that one person who really needs you may not come back to the light. So be brave and show your scars to the world. Your journey is someone else's survival guide, and they really need you more than you'll ever know.

HOME

Home is watching the waves crash on the shore, feeling the sun shine deep into my soul, and running with the sand between my toes. They said I would never get to go back home, but you called my name and didn't let me drown when I was swept away. You said I could always go back home because it is where I belong. My soul has been aching without you and now that I'm here, I have never been so alive. I found myself again.

She says out loud:
"Salt in my hair.
Sand on my toes.
Sun on my face.
I'm finally home."

ON THE ROAD AGAIN

We all hurt. We all bleed. We're all human. But there are those moments where you forget your limitations. Moments where you lift off, soar, and feel so alive. But then there are those moments where you never leave the ground. There are moments where the wind isn't strong enough, you crash, and you don't make it.

You were so confident. You believed the world was in the palm of your hand. "Not now," says life. "It's not your time," says Life. Life says you need to be more humble. You need to learn from failure. You need to understand you deserve absolutely nothing.

You have to try and try again. This is where a master succeeds. From failing so many times, it becomes second nature. This is where the second wind kicks in. A second chance at life to lift off. Do you feel the breeze? Are you strong enough to make it?

The first step is hardest getting back on the road of life. There's no one cheering for you on the side of the road. You have to make the decision to take that first step. Are you brave enough to take it? I promise, take one more step and you will never look back. Set yourself free from the pain, the failures, and the misery. You can make it if you believe.

Here's to you, the one who didn't give up, even when no one else believed. Hope is the only thing stronger than fear. There's no promise I won't crash again. That I will not fail again. But if you never try, you'll never know, and I have already lived with too many regrets.

Tell me no? I'll just push harder. You can't break me. If someone is going to break me, it's going to be me. This is my life, my rules, my destiny. Watch me fly, watch me fail. I don't care. Judge me, laugh at me. But I'd rather die knowing I tried my damnedest than live knowing I was too afraid to take one more step. See you on the road, kid. Let me know if you're down for a ride.

UNDERHERO

Ever get tired of watching the same story over and over? The hero saves the day. The underdog wins the game. Doesn't it get old after a while?

When you reach the end of a journey, you hope for the best. When you watch a comic book movie, you cheer for the hero. When you watch a sports movie, you cheer for the underdog.

Why can't that be you? Who is to say heroes are actors and not real? Who is to say the underdog can't come back and win? The battle? The war?

This isn't just about right or wrong or winning the game. It's about life. It's about your life. Are you giving it 100% everyday? Are you living your life to the fullest? Most importantly, do you believe in your dreams?

The hero and the underdog gives us hope. Holding onto hope may be the hardest thing you ever do. You fail. You fall. You lose. Hope is the glimmer of light in the path of darkness. You can be a hero. You can win the battle. Hold on tight to that glimmer and never let go. It will never get old if you believe that this is your destiny.

IMPOSTER HERO

Look in the mirror.
Do you like what you see?
What's her name?
What do they call her?
Who is she?
What do they say behind her back?
She said, "What do you mean, you're not superwoman?"
And I want to hyperventilate because part of me believes I tricked them,
But the other part of me is terrified of the responsibility,
The water that I carry keeps up this facade.
Or is it?
Am I a false prophet, walking around telling everyone that everything is going to be okay?
Can they see through my sunshine and rainbows?
You know, I don't actually know that.
I just know that it made me feel better when someone said that to me.
And when you're sad and alone, you seek reassurance and validation.
So is it a lie when I share that side of me with the world?
Is it so bad?
And then there are those moments you don't want to face the truth,
Not because you can't, but the other person cannot.
Is it a gift to let them down gently,
Have them believe they aren't a monster, while the truth eats at you like one inside?
Some people can't handle the truth, so when I was too afraid, too small, too triggered,
Am I condemned to be a monster like everybody else?
I WAS TOO TRIGGERED.
I WAS TOO SMALL.
I WAS NOT BRAVE ENOUGH.
HOW CAN THEY BELIEVE IN ME WHEN I AM SO FLAWED?

Why do we allow such a monster to live inside of our sacred bodies?
Why do we speak to ourselves without grace?
How can you feel that way?
Look at how far you've come.
Remember that little girl who was beaten.
Remember that little girl who was abandoned.
Why do you beat yourself down when you make a mistake?
How could you not give yourself some grace when you felt like you wanted to run away?
Everybody does.
Everyone has been hurt.
Everyone has been left behind.
Everyone makes mistakes.
Everyone needs grace.
Perfectly imperfect is the story to be told.
Raw, unfiltered, black and white.
Somewhere, the fearless one who raised her hand with confidence lost her way.
She started panicking when called on because she didn't want to be exposed.
Exposed for the imposter she was.
I thought I was Hermione Granger,
But then my heart was in my throat.
I couldn't speak.
If she couldn't love me,
How could they, if I was so not perfect?
I'm a different person now.
Now when they say, "Who is that woman?
The one that wears a silver chain around her neck?
It says "badass," but is she?"
Yes, yes she is.

Let your inner child nod and come back to life.
And when I said I was going to spend the rest of my life making people feel less broken?
Yes, I fucking am.
You can't be an imposter if you're human.
You were given a bar too high when you were programmed to believe perfection could buy you love.
You were given a bar too high when you believed killing yourself to get everything you could would be enough.
And now you're never satisfied, always looking for the next thing to fill a hole that should have never been created, the void of your heart.
The intrusive thoughts that walk with you like a shadow down the street.
There will always be shadow roaming around out there each time you're brave enough to face the world again.

Most real world heroes we never hear about, but the ones we do all know are glorified.
How many more versions of Spider-Man do we have to watch to believe in our own magic?
We all need hope and purpose.
We all need to believe in something more than ourselves.
But what if I told you that this painful journey is what defines you.
When you look in the mirror, you may see things you don't love, but my goodness, what a warrior.
Look at how she shines when the light hits her just right.
Look at her when she hits her stride and remembers that she may have bought that necklace, but she didn't earn it any less.
Why do we make these expectations feel bigger than ourselves?
Because we owe it to ourselves to jump as high as we can, reach for the stars, sing at the top of our lungs, and just be.
Embrace the moments that feel jarring and peaceful.
Embrace the opportunity to be the bigger person.
Maybe I'm an imposter hero, but the heroes that don't make the headlines are the ones that fill our souls with energy.
A mentor is a hero.
A friend who shows up for you is a hero.
A hero is simply defined as someone who is admired for their acts of courage.
Someone who was brave.
It is brave to show up for someone even if they're not always right.
Showing up is half the battle- and when you do for someone else- an act of defiant selflessness.
It is courageous when you realize that you are looked up to and you share your journey.
I may be an imposter hero, but I would have rather shared my story for the one- than for no one.
I may be imperfect, but I know there are people who walk this earth who believe I am perfect to them.
I may be flawed, but I am fucking beautiful- my heart, my soul, my power.

I cannot be defeated by the person that got me this far.
I cannot be defeated by the one person who has never let me down.
I'm still breathing.
I'm still here.
I'm still HER.
So please stop telling yourself you are anything other than enough.
When you hit play, they don't get to see what you see,
They see you in all of your glory.
The little things you diminish yourself with are nothing to them.
Let your replay be a celebration and an epiphany.
For you are exactly where you need to be.
For you are everything you need right now, in this very moment.
What do they say behind her back?
It can't be that she wasn't real.
It can't be that she wasn't brave.
It can't be that she wasn't courageous.
She poured heart out so there was still water to swim in.
She pushed herself to keep climbing, despite the pain and discomfort.
She claimed her place in this world.
It doesn't matter if they say imposter.
It doesn't matter if they say hero.
It matters what SHE says.
What SHE says.
I'm still breathing.
I'm still here.
I'm still HER.

PHOENIX RISING

She realized it was spring and time for the flowers to blossom again. She realized the last few months of fall and winter were just part of the journey … they did not define her. Things must die to be reborn again, and she knew it was her time. Time to rise again from the ashes. It was time to find her wings again and take flight. She whispers to herself, "get up."

As she stood, it was the tallest she had felt for a long time. Her slight smile confirmed the confidence rippling throughout her body like an electric current.

She was no longer afraid. The hours, days, and months ahead? She had walked and crawled them before. She shook her head. She knew what she wanted. She had failed before. She knew it could happen again, but she knew if she didn't try and keep trying she would never forgive herself.

With one deep breath, she started walking. One step at a time. She was shaky the first few steps. Her mind started to flood with fear of the past. "Keep breathing. Keep walking." She nodded. Her strides became more steady with each step. She looked up to the endless sky, longing to take flight. Walk before you run, run before you fly. She looked at the path ahead, and decided it was time to start jogging. It was time to be reborn.

HER 2.0

The ocean breeze gives me chilling goosebumps.
One might say from the cold, but not really.
I found your voice again across the Mediterranean Sea.
You called me and how I missed you.
For so long since we met, I've tried to find the meaning of words like home and love and family.
It took me all this time to learn it was never a place or another person or to belong.
For I came all the way to hear you again, but now I know you were with me all along.
You were in the stars that shone the way across the night sky.
For thousands of miles separated us, but that was just distance.
The feeling of home was deep inside a place that needed to be awakened.
It was the endless journey of finding HER, not Him, or them.
Community is the clutch we long for so we don't feel alone, but if we never found HER there would BE NOTHING.
They say "the greatest thing you'll ever learn is just to love, and be loved in return."
But I don't believe in return.
I say the greatest thing you'll ever learn is to love yourself.
You cannot keep giving without loving you first.
And when they say a house is not a home, it is not because you are alone.
It is only empty if the well you draw from is.
The world champions giving and giving and people will keep taking and taking if you don't find HER.
The roadmap is not clear, and you will lose your way many times.
This is because we cannot transform into our highest self without trials and tribulations.
The universe does not want us to suffer, it wants us to learn so that way we can give this earth our best work and selves.

The greatest stories of all time are not for the faint of heart.
We may not know of the greatest warriors who walked this earth because they look like everyday people.
This is why home and love and family are part of the journey.
There are times we must face the dragons alone, but if we believe in our magic, that this soul was meant to brave these high seas, we can do anything.
Her home, her love, her family was a slingshot of everything she exuded to the world.
Her strength, her kindness, her unwavering spirit, made others believe in their magic too.
It took me fifteen years to not come back home, to love or find family.
It took fifteen years to master the dragons that told her she didn't deserve any of them.
But now we know whenever there is light, you are always with us.
Now we know HER light is not just her own beacon, but the one that lights a path for others to find their HER too.
Blessed are those who never let their lights go out, HER fire will come and show the way home.

THE CYCLEBREAKER

I went for a ride to the other side
I passed places I once thrived
High school gymnasium
My second job
My best friend's house
I saw people who say they are so proud of me
That they love me
A caretaker who has known me for so long
But not her
She said she does
But she doesn't
She stopped when I started advocating for myself
And it really hurt me
I know this in my core
Because actions always speak louder than words
Why do they always demand blood?
Why can't my words be enough?
I lived it and no one else did
I get to decide that I'm the victim
And when someone comes to you
And shares their truth with you
Now there are always two sides of every story
And in my core, I know I see black and white more harshly than others,
But that doesn't mean I have a victim mentality
It just means I wish the world was a better place
So I'm not so afraid to have a child
I just want to leave this place better than I found it
And so many people aren't making it better
My enneagram type one makes me believe it's my job to fix that
And I don't know if I can
Rumi said, "Yesterday I was clever, so I wanted to change the world

Today I am wise, so I am changing myself"
But it's so hard when the people aren't always in your corner
I'm so tired of feeling alone
And fighting and advocating and championing myself
But it's not that I don't have them,
She just made me believe I didn't
So now when people say, "I'm proud of you"
So now when people say, "I love you"
It makes me feel so broken
Because this fight has been going on so long inside of me
I'm just so tired
Will this ever end?
And then when I watch Mitch Kessler gaslight Hannah
And make her an enabler instead of a victim
And how she couldn't live with that
I'm reminded of how I was never allowed freedom of speech
This country is screaming about protecting their rights
But what about the voices of the voiceless?
There are moments humans freeze
When we just can't
And this doesn't justify a damn thing
When people try to blame the victim
How about just not being a shitty person to begin with?
That would make the world a less fucked up place
Not be being stronger or better
But by not walking this world intentionally trying to hurt others
And I'm sorry
I'm sorry if you ever felt that was me
I had to be toxic because I was taught to be that way
I didn't know being passive aggressive was weak
I didn't know I wasn't good
Or as good as I could be
I was told I wasn't worthy
I believed it too
For so long

So I'm sorry if you witnessed a past version of me
While I didn't deserve to operate at such a low level,
I never meant to make you feel that way if I did
You see that's the difference
Hurt people hurt people
I'm sorry I hurt you
I am a hurt person trying to find my way
And it's not been a fun ride
It took much longer than I would like to admit
I assure you I'm more healed now
I assure you this version wants you to know how I would never want anyone to feel the way I did
And I hope I could never be capable of that
But I am human
And I am not perfect
And it took me a long time to even be okay with that
My toxic perfectionist masculinity was overwhelming
And now I'm so burnt out from being what I thought I had to
To climb out of this well that water kept me falling down into
Dreaming for the day I found the light
I just want to breathe like a normal person
I just want to process emotions like a normal person
I just want to sleep like a normal person
I just want to eat like a normal person
I just want to be like a normal person
I'm not important
I'm not special
But I hope to make you feel that way moving forward instead of anything else
I may be opinionated
I may be passionate
But I won't be like her
I won't be like her
Sometimes it's overwhelming
All the flashbacks

But I'm here now
Living in the same body
Reclaiming time and space
Wondering why I let so much time pass
Before I believed
No matter how small I was made to feel
I'm allowed to stand tall
I no longer apologize for the space I take up
The air I breathe
I'm not entitled to the space or the air,
But I want to believe I deserve something for the first time in my life.
And that I don't have anymore regrets moving forward
There are moments I froze
Those are the moments that make my chest hurt
Because I wanted things
And I couldn't ask
My throat closed up
My palms sweaty
My heart pounding
I was so scared to not be perfect
And I didn't believe I deserved more
But now I do
And I won't let HER down again
You may never get the apologies you believe you deserve,
But you can apologize
To yourself
To others
To people in your journey
And I hope when you find peace
I hope you find the beauty in the evolution
And if no one else is proud of you
I am
And if you can find peace with the fact that you are better today than yesterday
And try each day a little bit more

Then we win.
She doesn't.
Whatever he did to you doesn't.
We are better than that.
And I can live with that.
I hope you can too.
In fact, if you do this work.
If you keep climbing-
Through the trauma and the grief
And find this place of recovery.
I want to see you reclaim your place.
I want to see you fly.
And when you get there,
I hope you tell your story too.
I want to know that I'm not alone.
I want the cyclebreakers to have the platform they deserve.
I want them to get loud.
I want them to yell from the top of the mountains.
Maybe there needs to be a revolution.
Maybe there needs to be a resistance
I just want you to not feel so alone
I just want you to not feel like me
I broke the cycle.
And I still slip up.
I fall into grief.
I fall into trauma.
And it's exhausting- moving from one step the next only to fall down again.
I don't know how many more times we have to pick ourselves up and try to climb the mountain again.
My soul yearns for peace and quiet.
Maybe you were someone's Evil Queen.
But that doesn't define your whole story.
People say life is beautiful.
I'm not sure I have yet to fully understand,

But now I can look back and see more clearly.
Perhaps resurgence is watching karma do its job
It might take longer than we would like but
Sic semper tyrannis
It's always the whistleblowers who are treated like they're the problem
But it's the people in power who refuse to look in the mirror
I saw what you did and it wasn't okay
So when I became silent, you should have known the problem was you.
Thank you for the lessons
Thank you for understanding
Thank you for those who see beyond my imperfections
Thank you for those who really know me
Thank you for those humans who make the world a better place and believe I can do that too
He said one person doesn't matter if it's just one person
The majority doesn't rule karma
The universe does
So if you make a decision to not help one because the payoff isn't as big,
You will pay in karma.
That one person will never forget you didn't help them get up when they fell.
I was the one.
I was the underdog
And I got up over and over
Because I told myself to
And if I can help someone see that power within
If I can empower
Then I've won my friends
One person makes all the difference.
"Be the change you want to see in the world"
I know that was me.
Rising again
From the depths of grief and trauma

Finding recovery
Finding a platform to take off again
It's a beautiful life living so many different versions of yourself.
Be okay with each new phase finding who you are.
It's all meant to happen.
Be patient.
You will find this place.
It's coming.
I'll be there waiting to hear your story with a fresh cup of coffee.
I know you can do it.
This healing will take everything in you
It's going to hurt
You're going to sob
You're going to wish you didn't have to
Oh my dear, but you do.
This is where the wings are waiting for you
The goddess of victory has them for a reason
You have to be willing to fly
So the question you have to answer is
Do you want to stay where you are- or do you want to fly?
I want you to fly.
There's a place for you no matter how many times you find yourself facing the platform
No matter how many times you have to wait for the wings
There is always the wind waiting to help you take off
The universe is always watching
We are all rooting for you.
I want you to scream "I AM A CYCLEBREAKER"

So loudly
So proudly
And clap with the rest of the universe as you remember who the hell you are.
They always say I can't promise it will be easy, but it will be worth it.
And you are worth it.
Never forget how worthy you are.
2.0 is just the beginning.
There is so much more to do.

WORLD FULL OF COLORS

I want to live in a world full of colors.

A world where rainbows are honored for their beauty, not chastised for what they could represent.
I see colors of every kind and I'm grateful to walk in their presence.
I would never assume because someone is full of one color, or many, that they wouldn't deserve to walk among us.
For without all the colors, we could never see the world for what it really is.
A beautiful place not meant to be seen as black or white:

A beautiful masterpiece if we can remember everything is not about us, but is meant for everyone.
I stand with all the colors- may you shine brightly and never let those who cannot understand or do not want to dim your light.

CHOOSE LOVE

People are so weird about the word "love." I'm not really sure I ever understood love until I felt the impact I had on other people. Toxic love is when you give something and expect something back. Unconditional love is feeling seen, heard, and that you matter. You do things out of love, not out of fear. You don't worry about getting reciprocation because there is mutual respect. Love is kind as they say- what does kindness mean? Webster says "friendly, generous, and considerate." I say kindness is recognizing that someone else is a human being. That this human being may look different than me, think different than me, has different beliefs than me- but it doesn't matter. Because kindness recognizes that no one person is worth more than another life or that they have to be a certain way. That they deserve to be seen and heard and believed. Holding space for people is kind. Holding space for people is love. There is no more precious gift than our time. How do you want to be remembered? I choose love.

MAGIC

So many people believe in her magic now.
I think it's because I finally believe in her magic too.
Finding her took much longer than expected.
There was not a map leading the way.
That's because she was looking outside of herself for so long.
The power was always within.

The compass was always within.
The peace was understanding that home is wherever I'm with her.

The love was the empathy for the long, but necessary, journey to understand.
The light was the fire burning from the Phoenix within who broke the cycles.
I know now.
I love HER now.
And she will never be lost again.

"WEIGHTLESS"

"You make me feel weightless in a world that
has become so heavy"- JM Storm

As I faced the water again, I stood resolute with my feet firm in the sand.
This time, the waves would not get the best of me, so I had to figure out how to swim together.
Something about the water still drew me in, even though it reminds me of the worst parts of my life.
What was it that kept drawing me back in?
The best part about being in the water was feeling weightless.
That the burdens carried on my shoulders lifted like gravity, raising my body to the sky.
I finally knew what must be done.
The sounds of the ocean waves crashing over and over relentlessly was the sign.
Nothing is ever easy, even when it looks that way.
I was never one to succumb to the weight of the world, but it's been heavy for a long time now.
Eleven years old, I made a decision that I must survive.
That I would be complicit, silent, and accept the abuse in the walls of the place I called home.
One cannot understand the weight of the trauma until they're looking back and grieving.
Grieving the abuse did not stop, the pain endured in silence, and the acceptance that you did nothing because the punishment outweighed the risk.
This burden to carry is just like the relentless waves.
One wave crashing after the other.
The reminders are everywhere.
When you see someone with her haircut.
When you see someone with his car.

When you hear a voice that reminds you of them.
I didn't know it would take so long to stand in my power and speak my truth, but I did.
So while I may not be able to change the past or stop the waves from hitting, I can conjure the raindrops to ease the power of each crash by fighting the power it had over you.
I can stop the waves if I remember that I don't live there anymore.
I built a home where there is kindness, empathy, and love.
A place where no one has to be emotionally or physically abused because love leads the way.
There are no weapons- words or objects to be thrown- because compassion leads the way.
There is no walking on eggshells because everyone is loved and respected.
It may never be perfect, as humans could never inherently be, but it could be close.
It could be better than they were.
And if I must live with the noise of the waves crashing, it makes surviving easier to know I will never be like them.
There were a lot of things I was never allowed to feel, so I never knew what the good place would look like.
When you're in a bad place, you wonder what you did to deserve it.
That if someone who was supposed to love and protect you with everything they are could hurt you, it must have been your fault.
I have spent most of my life believing the bad, and believing that I could never be the good.
If they didn't, why would I?
I cannot waste another minute of my life thinking otherwise.
When you're a kid, you think before they tell you otherwise that you can be anything.
The naive energy that is a precious gift to the world because it reminds you of innocence.
When you take that away from a child, how could it not be defined as a mortal sin?

How can one reclaim their pedestal in this world after that kind of tragedy?
Or understand why the other kids were so much happier?
Or feel like they deserve to be here.
You have to have a toolkit to survive.

THE WORTHY 2.0 TOOLKIT

Step 1: Quiet the waves.

You didn't do anything wrong.

You didn't deserve to be treated like that.

Something is wrong with them, and now you get to choose who you are going to be.

Step 2: Break the cycle.

You don't want to be anything like them.

You don't want to speak to people the way you were spoken to.

You don't want people to make you feel the way you did.

You can do it.

You ARE worthy.

Step 3: This is hard.
Remember grace.
That you will wake up again feeling heavy.
It doesn't go away fully, so instead of carrying it, reclaim your place in the world by carrying it a bit better each day.
Find peace in the hard moments.
Remember to breathe.
You don't live there anymore.
You got out.
You don't have to see them again.
But when they appear in your thoughts, tell them they're not welcome.
This is your space.
You make the rules.
You live in a world that accepts you for everything you are.
And if you can do that a bit better each day, you have learned grace.
One shouldn't have to accept what happened to them, but they need to accept it did happen so one can move on.
We may never be able to fully process the trauma we live with, but we can make space for it where it no longer defines us.

Where it is a reminder of where you come from, but not your legacy.
One day the waves will bring you peace because you built a lifeboat and sailed the seas.
You're no longer drowning because you learned how to swim.
People will never fully understand how hard it was to keep your head above the water, but you do.
This is the only validation of your strength that you should need.
You are a cyclebreaker.
You're better than they ever could be.
The hardest things for us to live with are the moments we feel powerless.
We honor the former versions of ourselves we had to shed.
We remember that it's not our fault and should have never been put in those kinds of situations in the first place.
This is hard, but we love forward with grace and acceptance that we are in control of how we choose to let others treat us now.
We don't live there anymore.
We are reborn as worthy.

Worthy 2.0

Afterword

Thank you for being here with me.
I hope you find your teacher, your sister, your healer, and your safe one.
I know they're out there waiting for you.
You may cycle through different versions of each throughout your lifetime,
And that's okay.
The universe intends for this to be.
Just know those moments, those people are special.
They were meant to be part of the journey.
It's okay that not all of them are there forever.
They were there when they were meant to be there, and that's all that matters.
What matters the most is your well-being.
This journey has provided me with great reflection.
When I was a little girl, I didn't necessarily believe in magic, but I wanted to escape as much as possible.
I thought if you weren't tough or a tomboy, the world would eat you alive.
The only magic I found was escaping as a child to fantasy worlds, and really hoping there would be a more magical place for me one day.
It was often my only place I wanted to live in, but it was never in the land of the fairy tales as no one was coming to save me.
Now I understand that you can create your own magic and joy, and how evil it is to take that belief away from a child.

Regardless of our journeys in life, I hope we can all find the joy we deserve, that magic fills our days, and that regardless of the path- there is always a happy ending.
May your days have smiles that look like absolute, beaming joy like you are the sun itself.
What a journey this was, but I hope you know now that you were always worthy.
Here's to the next version of you.

So be it, so it is.

Worthy 2.0 Exercises

If you are unsure where to start your healing journey, the hardest part is making a decision that you are ready to move on and deserve to. You deserve to, dear one. And once you decide that you are worthy and ready, here are some helpful exercises that can help you prepare for the journey ahead:

Exercises:

1. APOLOGY LETTER TO SELF (reference page #93 A LETTER FOR MY BODY): I invite you to write a letter to yourself. Think about all the versions of yourself that you have cycled through your life since a child. Remember moments of shame and guilt and sadness. You don't have to carry this anymore. You don't live there anymore. Aren't you ready to release the past and live more in the present? Tomorrow is a beautiful day ahead. Tell your inner child what you will do better moving forward. You got this.

2. APOLOGY LETTER TO OTHERS (reference page #225 THE CYCLEBREAKER): As much as you believe you have been wronged and that is valid, it is quite possible that our best selves are not seen by others during this process. You may have unintentionally hurt others. Sometimes we do intentionally say or do things to hurt others because of the hurt we carry inside. You don't have to give them this letter, but think about people you've come across during

this journey. Release any anger, shame, disappointment, and frustrations. It's time to let them go.

3. BIRTHDAY LETTER TO SELF (reference page #202): Holidays can be challenging when the people who used to be there for you are no longer allowed. Isn't that something to celebrate? The growth? The journey? Reflect on the years that have passed. What are you most proud of? It doesn't matter how little the baby steps taken feel to you, they are still worthy of celebration. Happy birthday, beautiful soul. It's time to celebrate YOU!

4. BUILD YOUR ARCHETYPE AFFIRMATIONS: Which of the archetype resonated the most with you? Are you a Cyclebreaker? Are you a Phoenix? Are you a Black Sheep? Maybe, you are all of these things. I invite you to create affirmations that empower you to live these truths each and every day. I AM WORTHY is a great way to start.

5. TELL YOUR STORY: This book started as journals as a child. As time advanced, so did technology and I started making notes on my iPhone. The combination of these efforts is what you see here today. Maybe right now journaling is where you are most comfortable. Maybe it's updating your social media accounts. Tell your story. There are people out there who need to know they are not alone. This book came from a place of great loneliness and wanting to ensure that others never felt that way. I'm proud to tell this story. I look forward to hearing yours.

Thank You

It's incredibly challenging and difficult to be raw and authentic in today's world. This journey bares my soul to the world and exposes me. I expect some to appreciate the vulnerability and I expect others to want to deny or cancel how brutal the reality of it all was. This book is the ending of a cycle for me. The one I knew I had to break and have been working so hard towards. I want to thank my healers, my mentors, my tribe and most importantly, my sister, who has lived this story with me and graciously helped me tell my story. Thank you to my new friends who have joined me on this journey. I look forward to the next one with all of you. May your days of trauma and grief be few and far between and may your recovery and resurgence inspire the world. So be it, so it is.